STO
FRIENDS OF ACPL
W9-BNZ-707

MAY 19 '76

THE NEW
FEMINISM

Fifty years after they won the right to vote, women in America again mobilized their energies in an effort to gain equal rights in our society. The new movement for women's liberation had taken root. Lucy Komisar, a leading feminist, has created a book uniquely sensitive to the problems of today's youth in relation to this movement. This is a book written not only for young people but with them, for *The New Feminism* includes actual rap sessions with young men and women who discuss the roles assigned to them by society, their feelings about these roles and themselves, and their views of the women's liberation movement.

Where do the concepts of "masculinity" and "femininity" begin for each of us? Where did they begin in terms of our society and even of the world? What does it mean to be born female? How have women been viewed in history? What do anthropological studies show of women's roles throughout the world? What are the subtle and blatant forms of discrimination women face? What are the implications for you? These are some of the issues dealt with in *The New Feminism.*

*"Sex prejudice has been the chief hindrance in the rapid advance of the women's rights movement to its present status, and it is still a stupendous obstacle to be overcome. This world taught woman nothing skillful and then said her work was valueless. It permitted her no opinions and said she did not know how to think. It forbade her to speak in public, and said the sex had no orators. It denied her the schools, and said the sex had no genius. It robbed her of every vestige of responsibility, and then called her weak. It taught her that every pleasure must come as a favor from men, and when to gain it she decked herself in paint and fine feathers, as she had been taught to do, it called her vain."*

*Carrie Chapman Catt, 1902*

*Franklin Watts, Inc., 845 Third Avenue, New York, N.Y. 10022*

"Sonnet XXXI" which appears on page 82 is from *Collected Poems,* Harper & Row. Copyright 1923, 1951 by Edna St. Vincent Millay and Norma Millay Ellis. By permission of Norma Millay Ellis.

"Lines to Mr. Bowdle of Ohio" which appears on pages 94 and 95, by Alice Duer Miller. By permission of Denning Miller, holder of the copyright.

"Domesticity" by Kay Reinartz, which appears on page 158 is reprinted by permission of the author.

*The principle sources for the facts and statistics that appear in this book were government publications, newspapers, and journals, newsletters, and books that deal with women and the feminist movement.*

SBN 531-01981-0
Copyright © 1971 by Lucy Komisar
Library of Congress Catalog Card Number: 70-149011
Printed in the United States of America
1 2 3 4 5 6

1900181

*To my mother and father who made it very clear that brains were not doled out on the basis of sex and always expected me to be at the top of my class.*

# TABLE OF CONTENTS

THE NEW
FEMINISM

# CHAPTER ONE
# WHAT IS SEXISM?

"Ships and snails and puppy dogs' tails. . . . sugar and spice and everything nice. . . ."

How early in life did you learn about the "differences" between boys and girls? When did you first discover that boys are supposed to like climbing trees and playing baseball and exploring empty lots while girls pretend to be little mommies with dolls and embroidery and miniature stoves?

When girls and boys grow up, they become the new generation's imitation of their parents. Did you ever even question the idea that a woman's job is to take care of her husband and her children while a man goes out to work and supports his family?

Did you ever wonder why women who work are often secretaries and nurses while men are bosses and doctors? Why the United States government is run by men, why women in state and federal legislatures are an oddity, why your town's mayor is probably a man, why most judges are men, why radio announcers are usually men—in fact, why, of the majority of jobs that are done in the world by men and women, the most important, prestigious, and well-paying jobs are done by men?

The system of dividing up the roles people play in society and setting them in separate categories called "male" and "female" is called sexism. It is saying that women are less intelligent than men, it is believing that men should be aggressive and women passive, it is thinking that being female uniquely qualifies a person to do housework, it is asserting that a husband's work is more important than a wife's.

The struggle for women's liberation is a struggle against the "sex-role system" which insists that the physical differences between men and women, which should be relevant only to the part each plays in reproduction, ought, in addition, to restrict their opportunities in areas of life that have nothing to do with sex.

The battle against sexism is not new. If you had been born a woman one hundred years ago, you might have been caught up in the struggle for the right to vote, to control your own earnings and property, and to work at being something other than a teacher, a factory worker, a maid, or a prostitute.

Today, the issue has been drawn still more sharply. Even feminists —people who favor equal rights for women—of a hundred years ago accepted the notion that a woman's role included housekeeping and child care. Today's feminists declare that women cannot be equal to men until everyone shares these tasks. Why, they ask, should children be allowed to interrupt a mother's career but not a father's?

The demands of the women's liberation movement include equality in jobs and education, beginning with the same opportunities as men for admission to schools and colleges, the chance to work at challenging jobs, and the opportunity to receive the same pay as men who do similar work.

Women want government-supported child-care centers so that their children will be well cared for. They want the repeal of laws which restrict the right to abortion so that no woman will be forced to bear children against her will. They seek the end to legal restrictions on women's rights in laws that pertain to business, government, the family, and criminal codes. And they are attempting to change the image of woman as a compleat housekeeper, child rearer, sex object, who is defined by her femininity more than by her humanity.

Sexism is not something that affects only adult men and women—it limits, channels, and defines the lives of boys and girls from the time they are just toddlers. The newest part of the movement has been the emergence of groups of high school students who are concerned about the effects of sexism on their own lives and about their futures as adults in the world outside school.

Some of these young women have formed groups to talk about the ideas of feminism and about the particular conditions in their own lives that confine them to a second-class status. They are also aware of how the system hurts men by forcing them to live up to "masculine" ideals that are just as false as the "feminine" ones.

High school and junior high school girls were brought together to talk about the issues of women's liberation that touch their lives—and a group of high school boys gathered separately to discuss the same topic. Their concerns and opinions focus on questions that affect every teen-ager in America today—for all young people will have to face the problems and the decisions that these teen-agers talked about.

# CHAPTER TWO
# TEEN-AGERS TALK ABOUT THEMSELVES

Debbie is sixteen and a high school student in a large American city: "If you've ever looked in a playground and watched little kids play, you see that the boys have the fire engines and the girls have the tea sets. I was watching my cousin who is a girl, and she said, 'Why can't I ride the fire engine? I'm just as good, I can ride it.' And the boy wanted to play with the tea set. But the point is, it sounded so out of place! Like, she's not supposed to do that and he's not supposed to do that. But why not?"

Laren is fifteen: "When I was in junior high, the boys always got shop—they got printing and machine shop and woodworking. I always wanted woodworking, I liked woodworking, but we got cooking and sewing."

Wendy, age sixteen and out of high school: "Even in elementary school, the boys would go swimming in the morning, and the girls would sit and sew aprons and things."

Debbie: "I used to think that you had to be a boy to really understand about mechanical drawing and machine parts. I had been saying all year that girls shouldn't take it, only boys should. Now I take it all back. I was talking to some of the boys, and they are as ignorant as we are."

Judy is fifteen and a student at a special high school for science and math: "I just assumed when I came into drafting that I would do badly. Everybody had told me how terrible it is and how only the boys do well. You just accepted it that boys always know how to put things together—that they see things with a different eye than girls. So I really accepted it. It's kind of disgusting!"

One of the girls acted to protest against the system. Elizabeth, fourteen and a ninth grader in junior high school: "I complained in my home economics class. They give cooking and sewing to all the girls and printing and carpentry and electronics to the boys. I asked why the girls couldn't take some of the crafts, and the teacher said that cooking is for girls and electronics is for boys. Oh, there's also one other thing that girls can take—child care. They learn how to make toys for children and instant pudding for babies.

"And in sewing class, when you're not sewing, the teacher gives you books that show you how to set tables and how to make meals that men like, and they tell you always to be a good listener!"

Madeline is twelve and an eighth grader in the suburbs: "I started German this year. We got a first-grade German book, and suddenly it all came back to me. The first sentence was, 'Mother is shopping, Heidi is painting, and Fritz is flying his airplane.' Everyone is doing what he is supposed to do—of course father isn't mentioned until he comes home from work for supper."

Elizabeth: "We have to start all over again from the beginning. Everything in the books we read has been written by men. The only women I can recall are either tyrants like Queen Victoria and Betsy Ross, or they're somebody's wife."

Laren: "I never learned about the suffragists in school."

Madeline: "Women just simply aren't mentioned. Like in the movie we saw about John Fry who was an early revolutionary. When John Fry came home for the day, his wife was finishing cooking him dinner. They didn't mention anything about his wife, and I'm sure nobody noticed that his wife hadn't done anything besides cook dinner in the whole film."

Judy: "We learned something about women's role in World War I; they made bandages and things like that. It's only recently that I've started to think about it at all. I never thought about women, really."

Paula is fifteen and an activist in women's liberation: "I was under the impression that there simply were not any famous women writers or artists, and that is why we didn't learn about them. And that's part of it—there are too few of them."

Wendy: "Magazines, movies, television—all reinforce the stereotypes of male and female. When you look in the magazines that are supposed to be for our age groups, *Seventeen* and *Mademoiselle,* they show you these fantastically glamorous "feminine" models that you're supposed to look like."

Liz is thirteen and a ninth-grade student at a high school of art and design: "Teen magazines—the teen love and true confessions are terrible too. I remember one where a girl who was considered a tomboy was in love with this guy. She got herself some sexy clothes, and he took her out. Then she saved someone from drowning, and he left her! But just as he was leaving, she began to cry, and he came back because *only real girls cry!*"

Madeline: "You see it on television also. The epitome of the situation comedy on television is 'I Love Lucy.' Of course Lucy is a very stupid person and so is Ethel; Fred is so old he's no good either. But Ricky is masculine and takes care of them all and goes off to work and is brighter than anyone else. Lucy naturally stays home with the baby."

Liz: "One of the worst is 'Leave It to Beaver.' The wife is in the kitchen all the time and leaves all the decisions to the husband. She is always the one that gets upset and emotional, and he is always cool."

Elizabeth: "Our mothers get it too. One of the articles in *Family Circle* was 'How to Raise Your Son to Be a Real Man.' It said men and women should not compete with each other in front of the children. They should assume their proper roles."

Beth is fourteen and a ninth grader—and Madeline's sister: "Girls put down their own intelligence. They giggle. Not so much with other girls, but when they are in front of boys. They have to act as if the boys are better than they are, because that is the way things are supposed to be. Girls are supposed to be little and meek and not know too much."

Madeline: "One teacher asked a question of one of the quiet girls who sits on one side of the room, and she answered, 'Gee, I don't know' and looked at this boy like, 'Was *that* okay?' It was terrible! It was obvious she didn't know because she wasn't supposed to know much, and the boy should answer that for her, please."

Beth: "In our social studies class, on the whole, the girls just don't say *anything*. They sit there. In math, if they get a different answer on something, they immediately assume that they're wrong instead of the other person being wrong. They're just not very assertive about anything."

Judy: "Debbie and I were the only girls in our class who made Stuyvesant (a special New York high school for science and math, open only to boys until a court decision in 1969). The other girls in our class were all so accustomed to playing the role of the woman. I couldn't understand it—they didn't have any ambition. The boys in my class wanted to be scientists and things like that, and they all made it—every single one of them made Stuyvesant. I think the girls didn't because they were never encouraged."

Elizabeth: "I can remember my mother telling me that it's not good to do things as well as a man does. She said that men don't like it—that men want to win. And if you want to get one, then you have to lose. I said I didn't believe in that, and both my parents replied, 'Well, then you're never going to get married.' "

Laren: "In school we had guidance, and when it came to graduation time, they had job opportunities and job counseling and things like that. The counselors would say, 'Well, maybe you boys would be interested in being a lawyer, and that kind of thing, and they would recommend nursing school for the girls. It sort of bothered me, but it was accepted. I guess it's pretty accepted because you know the whole society works around it."

Wendy: "I went to an all-girl school, and they had a regular curriculum, but there were special kinds of courses that people out of the neighborhood could go for—and the only things they offered were nursing and home economics, the traditionally female things."

Beth: "Most women just don't think as big as most men. I think that's the major problem. People used to think that I was insane because I'm very aggressive and on top of that I have some wild ideas for my own career. I'll probably become some kind of political scientist or psychologist or biologist. A lot of people think you're not supposed to do that, because you're a girl. You know, girls become nurses and teachers.

"When I was very little, I really had high ambitions, and people used to bug me about it. For a while I sort of worried: maybe there's something wrong with me, maybe I'm wrong being so ambitious. When I was nine, I wanted to run for a seat in the Senate! And one of my very best friends said to me, 'How can you raise a family? If you run for the Senate won't it interfere with your kids and your husband?'

"But what if they said that about men? Maybe men shouldn't have careers, because they don't have enough time for their wives and children. I think many men don't have enough time for their families and should spend more time with them. I think most women are too tied to them. I'd favor the idea of both men and women having part-time jobs and sharing in the house and bringing up the kids. I think it would be psychologically more healthy for the kids, too, if they had close relationships with both parents."

Madeline: "Nobody liked the idea of me being a brain surgeon. I wanted to be one, I guess since I was eight. The reaction was 'Ha, ha, that's funny, that's cute. The little thing wants to be a brain surgeon.' Then it changed to, 'Well, she's a very smart young lady.' And then it changed to, 'But you're so nice in music, my dear.' "

Debbie: "My parents wanted me to be a lawyer. Three hours ago, before I came here, I said to myself, a lawyer? That's a man's job! But now I'm thinking about it. Why is it a man's job? Why shouldn't I be one?"

Wendy: "My friend and I graduated in January and found out that when girls try to get jobs, they just can't get anything except typing. The only jobs we could get was working at the telephone company or as a secretary someplace. My friend tried to work at a bookstore, but they wouldn't hire her because she was a girl. They came right out and said it!

"The whole dream is to catch a rich man and to make yourself beautiful so you can get him. Instead of concentrating on themselves as people and fulfilling themselves in what they'd [women] like to do, it's a matter of becoming some*thing* so somebody else will want them."

Judy: "I want a family, but I want something that's not with my family—that I can enjoy and feel that I'm important. I couldn't just wash dishes and diapers all my life. I would feel my life was wasted. I'd look back and say 'What did I do?' "

Laren: "My mother says that often—that she feels she's wasted part of herself. She's very intelligent and she could have gone to college and worked. But she didn't, and I know she's sorry."

The psychological damage caused by sexism is more subtle but just as harmful as the outright discrimination it promotes. One of the most difficult problems for girls—and boys—is living up to the stereotyped ideals of femininity or masculinity the sex-role system has fostered.

Judy: "I was using some liquid to clean my hands in printing and I just poured it on over me. The teacher yelled at me in front of the boys, 'Judy, you should know better; that's not feminine. You should put it on a piece of cotton and dab it on.' "

Paula: "Are you kidding?"

Judy: "I don't think he was kidding. I said I didn't think it was such an unfeminine gesture."

Paula: "I think that femininity and masculinity are learned, and none of it is natural."

Laren: "I think there is a difference between femininity and daintiness."

Judy: "I still am wrapped up in the word 'femininity.' When I think of it, I probably would think of Tricia Nixon. She wears very feminine dresses, and she seems like the type that always does the right thing and always knows the right fork to use. She is probably a very charming girl—I don't know her. She just looks so perfect. You never can see her messy."

Paula: "In the seventh and eighth grades, I used to get up on the stage when we had our drama class and go dancing around, and I used to be a tomboy. I remember my sister one day took me aside and told me to walk like this, with small little steps. She said I looked like a boy."

Judy: "In the beginning of the year our homeroom teacher told us not to wear pants because we would look masculine. And when Laren came in pants, she made her march up and down in front of the room; she really embarrassed her."

Beth: "I wear blue jeans, and you're not supposed to. The girls wear these shiny frilly blouses. You can see them for miles away."

Madeline: "If they hit the light at the right angle you're blinded for life! Would you like to take a feminine and masculine test? First, how do you look at your nails? Now light a match. Now blow it out. Now drink this glass of water. *That* was feminine, *that* was masculine. I've gotten this test about three times. If you're feminine you're supposed to drink it very slowly, if you're masculine you're supposed to slug it down. If you're feminine you cross your knees like that, and if you're masculine, cross them like that. The first time I did a lot of things 'wrong,' but after the person told me 'this is masculine and this is feminine,' I got them all right because of course I know what I'm supposed to do if I want to be feminine."

Wendy: "I used to think femininity was frills and lace and being sweet and quiet. Now I guess it is just that you are physically and biologically a woman. And the same for masculinity. I used to think it meant aggressive and strong. Now I think it's just the biological definition.

"In high school all the women gym teachers were supposed to be dykes [lesbians], which is a very old stereotyped idea of women gym teachers. Because they're physically fit, and they're strong, and they can do all sorts of things with their bodies, and that's supposed to be masculine, I guess."

Madeline: "You can be a cheerleader, because then you're backing up the man."

Beth: "There's this particular boy in my social studies class who is very reactionary, and I'm very radical, and we're both very verbal. We spent the whole year arguing; it was a class joke. Well, once they were going to put one of us on the debating team, and the teacher said, 'I think boys can debate better than girls, because girls sound unfeminine when they raise their voices and make aggressive statements.' To me, that's ridiculous. I think I can debate better than he can, and I don't care what you say about my sex—I think I can do a better job."

Winning the competition for a boy is often thought to be a girl's highest achievement, more important than receiving good grades in school or planning a future; but some girls are beginning to think that this competition destroys real relationships between girls and boys.

Wendy: "There was always this rivalry between two girls. They would be very close and all of a sudden, if they decided they liked one boy, their friendship would break up."

Beth: "What I find most offensive is that they are so preoccupied with makeup and clothes. It's their major interest. And the kids who are not interested just in makeup and clothes are snubbed.

"I think the biggest problem in junior high is that, because there's such a great big thing about women being inferior, a lot of boys won't just be really friends to girls. They just use them as status symbols."

Wendy: "Because boys always have to be more aggressive, if you're really aggressive and friendly, they take it that you want to have a sexual relationship, and they can't meet you on any other basis than sex."

Madeline: "I was having a political discussion with a boy, and whenever I made some point that he thought put him in a bad position, he called me a 'little lady'!"

Debbie: "The funny thing is that a lady is supposed to be like 36-24-36. You know, the really shapey ones. I was talking today to some boys, and they said, 'I can't wait until you turn eighteen.' I said, 'What do you mean you can't wait until I turn eighteen?' 'Because you'll be beautiful,' they said. What does that mean? Until I'm eighteen I'm not beautiful? Maybe I don't have a figure now—until I'm eighteen I won't have this beautiful shape that they call a woman or femininity? Until then I'm just a plain ordinary human being that could be placed in the category of a man? That they couldn't care less? I'm not a woman until I'm eighteen? It's not fair."

Wendy: "When I walk down a street, I check it out to see how many men are on one side and how many are on the other to see which way I'll get least harassed. I used to be very insecure about that, and then I found out that everyone else does that also."

Liz: "If you just walk down the street you have to be aware. The behavior of men toward women—women keep their eyes ahead, and they don't look. When I'm with a man, I stare back. I talk back. I say, 'Can I help you?' "

Beth: "One thing that bugs me is that I can't ask a boy for a date, and I don't like that at all. There's one boy that I really like and I'd really like to get to know better, but according to the official social rules, I just have to wait and flirt and hope for the best, which is a bad deal. I think it's important to be able to go ask boys for dates, to go after them as friends, instead of just waiting."

Elizabeth: "I called up a boy once. The whole school talked about it for weeks. He was okay on the phone, but the next day he went around the whole school telling everybody. It was to build his own ego. My mother said that girls are not supposed to be aggressive."

Debbie: "I'm ashamed to admit it, but I always put myself lower than the boy I go out with. If he wants to go someplace, even though I hate it, I'll go with him because he asked me to. When a boy asks me out, I let him make the decisions. I feel that I can't make the decisions. I have that inferiority complex which is very bad."

Judy: "I was thinking about—like, who pays? If I go out with a guy, I wouldn't pay for myself. And then I was thinking, I probably have more money than he does. I usually do. And is it right for him to pay for you, because the other way is supposed to hurt his ego. I'm sure a lot of people have that problem. And you don't know whether to ask, so usually you just let them pay. In fact, almost always."

Debbie: "Yes, you take a bus instead of a taxi, because you're afraid that he hasn't got enough for the taxi, or you order the least-expensive thing; or you pick a movie over a play, because the play is more expensive."

Judy: "If the women's liberation movement thinks women should be equal with men, then girls ask boys out, boys ask girls, girls pay for boys, right?"

Judy: "How can you ever know who your real self is. If you're always playing roles to suit society, then you'll never know. You have to play the role. Like, when the man comes home, the woman gets the dinner and the slippers and the pipe and the newspaper and they settle down and *she's* knitting."

Madeline: "We had a Christmas party. All the girls were standing over by the food and serving the boys the drinks and cutting up the cakes. So this boy went over to do it, and the other boys said, 'No, let the girls do it; they're better at it.' It kind of made me sick."

Beth: "I think that women have the potential to perform jobs just as well as men do. They don't have to have children, and they certainly don't have to spend their lives caring for them. They can be just as useful in other ways. We have so many children in the world already with the population boom that there's no necessity for them to have children.

"Women don't think enough about the future. They sort of say, 'I'll get married and the future will take care of itself.' If they do decide to become mothers, they won't have anything really interesting to offer their kids. And if they don't have children, they just won't have anywhere to go if they don't have a profession or at least some kind of interest, something to pursue."

Paula: "I think it doesn't really matter if a woman is a housewife as long as the housewife role isn't considered in a different light than her husband's job and if she could go into the business world and her husband could be a 'housewife' without everyone snickering as everyone did in my class when Mr. Rabinowitz was talking about tribes where women were the chiefs."

Wendy: "Even when you're in school, in elementary school, all the teachers are women and as you get into the upper grades, there are more men teachers; especially in science and math, most of the teachers are men. You sort of begin to associate taking care of children with women. If a woman wants to have kids—like I really like kids but I'm not sure I want to have one—I don't think there should be any differentiation between which parent takes care of the kids. They should share it."

Judy: "I think it's the way it is because women like to take care of the details more. No—I can't even say, because I'm so conditioned to how life is now. I'm so conditioned that I'm all mixed up. I don't know if it's the role or that women really like to take care of the details of taking care of babies, and men don't like it. Men seem to like to hold a baby, but they'd rather that women take care of all the details. Do most of the men like what they're doing now?"

Paula: "I have a friend, Steve, and we were talking, and he said if we ever got married, he wanted to take care of the children and I would work. And that's good, because I think if Steve wants to take care of his children, he should."

Judy: "You can both do it together. You can bring kids to day-care centers for half a day while you both work, and when you come home, you can take care of them together."

Laren: "I'd like to be with my child."

Judy: "What about the man? He should have the opportunity too."

Laren: "I didn't say that. Together. I think he should share it also. It's a joy. It shouldn't be a chore."

The girls got into the effect of the male/female stereotypes on the boys they knew.

Wendy: "Do stereotypes hurt boys? Yes. It was kind of like if a boy did something that could be construed as being feminine, it was 'Oh, ho, ho, he's a fag [male homosexual],' or something like that. And that was supposed to be some horrible thing."

Beth: "Boys try to act super-tough. I know this boy and when he's by himself and not with a lot of other people, he's just a very sweet, quiet type of kid, very nonaggressive. He used to be really nice, but more and more I think he became very ashamed of this pacifism and now he's got this really phony he-man attitude. He even joined the football team. He's not accepting himself as the person he really is. When he's not with a lot of people, he's still very quiet and very sweet, but whenever he's with a group, he becomes very nervous, very fidgety, and at one point he had this pair of dark glasses, and whenever he'd go into public he'd put them on and start talking very loud. I just get the feeling the whole thing was a put-on."

Do boys agree with the feelings expressed by the girls? Some boys *are* sensitive and aware of what girls in women's liberation are trying to say—and they add some special viewpoints of their own about how the system bothers *them*. These boys are all students or new graduates of Stuyvesant High School in New York. What follows is some of their thoughts and responses to questions asked them.

Neal is eighteen: "I was on the student-faculty committee at Stuyvesant and from what I saw, the administration was dead set against any girls coming in. Our principal is a guy with pretty archaic views. He's always had guys there, and he's used to the situation, and he wanted to keep it that way. I remember when Alice di Rivera won the court case, he wouldn't speak to anyone for a couple of weeks, and he made an overt effort to get as few girls as possible. This year we were told there were going to be about thirteen other girls for the second year, not the two hundred and fifty the Board of Education dictated to us.

"In high school, of course, there's the tracking system. Girls are tracked into home economics courses and generally not technical courses. That was one of the things that the girls were up against when they wanted to go to Stuyvesant—that it was a technical school. And they didn't give them shop courses there; they gave them a special arts program."

Roland is eighteen: "As soon as a child is born, it gets pink clothes or blue clothes. You're already marked. Everything extends from there. It's little girls who get to make the cakes and cookies and boys who go out and play baseball. When you look at sports men are always better than women. I wonder whether that's hereditary or learned.

"There are thousands and millions of social rules which come up. Girls are supposed to be feminine. The word 'feminine' is a very important word, and it's defined as pink and boys carrying books and holding doors, the double sex standard—boys can do things girls can't. It's a ludicrous system. It's a pain to run for a door, and who wants to carry extra books unless someone else is physically unable to carry them. And I like pink, and if I wear pink to school, it becomes a pain."

The boys thought about how the myths of what it is to be "masculine" hurt them. They discussed their own feelings about masculinity.

Bob is sixteen: "It's being six foot three, two hundred and twenty pounds, with bulging muscles. The guy who can weight-lift eight hundred pounds, he's masculine, and the feminine one is a girl who's got the good figure and is beautiful."

Roland: "That's not all. Just because you have a good body for a girl doesn't necessarily mean you're feminine. It has to do a lot with the whole way you carry yourself, the whole attitude you take toward life.

"And you don't have to be a five-hundred-pound football player to be considered masculine; men have the power, so that's their symbol of masculinity. If you're weak and servile, then you're not really considered masculine."

Neal: "I think what has replaced all that now for men is the job, the family, and money. That's the substitute now. It seems to me that the whole competitive aspect for men is very oppressive. My first reaction is to get out of it as much as possible."

Bob: "They're all false standards of masculinity, and I don't care if I live up to them or not. It doesn't mean a thing to me."

Roland: "We *say* that."

Neal: "I do care. I did for four years. I maintained the average. I did the work. I did all those things that were expected of me as a male student."

Roland: "I care, too, but I'm trying harder to eliminate this, because I don't think it's right. It's very difficult, and there are a lot of things I do unconsciously, and I'm not even aware of them now. It's hard to adjust to the fact that you're losing some of your power."

They were all aware of the stereotyped image of women presented in the media.

Neal: "One of the things I notice now is that I'm more aware when I watch television or read a magazine. The media is disgusting. The television—when they get on there with those advertisements for the little kids' toys—the situation comedies are especially bad. They're really incredible, and they really tend to cement the roles. People watch a lot of television; it's shaping a lot of values."

Roland: "There's exploitation of men as well as women. Magazines like *Playboy*. It's not only the naked girls, but it's also the cool playboy of the month. You know—How many girls has he made this month?

"Two weeks ago women's liberation sponsored an ogle-in that was very interesting. I wasn't aware that women were really degraded by the fact that when they walk down the street, men whistle at them and say, 'Hey baby, what's happening?' I thought it was sort of complimentary. Judy explained it was really degrading; it's harassment."

Neal: "I couldn't understand that women couldn't go out on the street alone. Women can't go out on the street because they're constantly harassed, bothered. I noticed this with Ellen. I was working the other night—I work in an ice-cream store—and Ellen came to pick me up. It was ten minutes before I had to get off, and she was standing in front of the counter and everybody who came in, guys just bothered her and whistled at her and looked her up and down. That bothered me. It happened because she wasn't with me. If I had been walking down the street with her she wouldn't have been bothered."

The boys were enthusiastic about the implications of feminism for dating habits.

Neal: "That was the first thing I thought about when I heard about women's lib. I said, 'Oh, that's great. I'm really tired of this, maybe now girls will be more aggressive.' "

Roland: "Boys are expected to be the initiators in all social relationships with girls. You're supposed to start things, you're supposed to say hello. You're supposed to ask for dates. You're supposed to call up. It's a burden, you know."

Arthur is sixteen: "It's a bother that the boy has to make all the advances. And if a girl comes up to a boy, everybody looks upon her as some kind of loose girl or just some kind of oddball."

Bob: "It would be a lot easier for both male and female if it were a lot more spontaneous. It's expected for me to ask a girl for a date. If it were spontaneous for her to ask me or me to ask her, it would cause a lot less hassle."

Roland: "And you pay for the girl, and you end up seeing half as many movies as you want that way."

Neal: "There's always this defense, though. You have to defend the woman you're with."

Roland: "And when you take a girl out, you have to take her home; she doesn't take you home. Though that's not one I'm sure of, because it seems to me most men *are* stronger than most women."

Neal brought up another role habit that infuriates most women.

Neal: "When I go into a situation where I meet another guy I sometimes ignore the girls there. I went over to Eric's house the other night, and I started talking to him about my job for about fifteen minutes, and I completely ignored Ellen. I didn't realize it until she pointed it out to me."

They talked about the roles of men and women in adult life. Is it the man's job to be the breadwinner?

Neal: "No, I don't think so. I think that's just one of those things that's been handed down. At one point it might have been necessary for the woman to be at home constantly bearing children, not being able to choose *when* she wanted to bear children or *if* she wanted to have them, and the men had to go out hunting or whatever, but now that's really archaic; there's no need for that."

Roland: "There are obviously physical differences and if you have a pregnant woman, she can't go out and help you on the hunt, but now it's a different society and it's much easier to equalize and eliminate these differences."

Bob: "It's also the whole society that plays on the ego, that if the man isn't the breadwinner, everyone else gets down on him and his ego becomes deflated, because he feels inferior. It's the whole thing of egos being played upon where one has to be better than the other and has to fulfill a role that is almost predestined."

Roland: "There's that old idea that women don't have to go to college because they can just as easily survive on what the man makes. I mentioned that to a girl once. I said, 'You don't have to worry about that. You're going to get married.' She got really offended."

Arthur: "The traditional roles should be changed. What we have now is not terribly fulfilling where the male plays one role and the female plays another role. I don't think either of them should stay home and take care of kids."

Bob: "My mother can't stand it. The only reason she stayed a housewife for the past twelve years is because my sister comes home for lunch every day from grammar school. Now my sister will be in junior high school next year, and my mother's going out and working."

Should men share housework?

Bob: "My father does it all the time. He washes the dishes every night, and I do the drying."

Neal: "My father does part of the housework, but I still think there's an unfair distribution because they both work. When I think of it, my mother's job is the harder. She has to take care of a lot of kids. She does the wash. My mother went back to school about eight years ago, and my little brother was four years old then. She went through this big crisis, and she finally went back, but she felt so guilty. She still feels very, very guilty about the whole thing—she feels that she wasn't a mother."

# CHAPTER THREE GROWING UP A GIRL

What is it like to grow up as a girl in this society?

You start out with pink ribbons and the insistence by all your parents' friends and relatives that you are destined to be Miss America of 19??. (If you were a boy, you would get blue ribbons and the prophecy of being our country's greatest president.)

When you begin to toddle, and learn to talk, you find out that you are a "little lady," that you are pretty and sweet and cuddly—a perfect baby girl. (Boys, of course, are little men. It has been discovered that they do not get cuddled as much as girls; they are taught to be independent early.)

Now you are three, four, or five and beginning to explore your surroundings. But don't get dirty or tear your pretty starched dress. Don't play rough or throw a ball—your dolls and tea sets are more proper toys. Meanwhile, boys are beginning to find out about the real world by climbing over rocks and poking into fields and lots and perhaps getting their faces dirty and their clothes torn, but at the same time sharpening their spirit of discovery and adventure.

Psychologists have said that the ability to think analytically depends largely on the degree to which a child is encouraged to take the initiative and solve his or her own problems. Girls are protected more than boys and suffer more restrictions—and as a result their intellectual ability is damaged at the very beginning of their lives.

By first grade, you have already learned that there are big differences between girls and boys. And in school they are magnified. Girls and boys stand in different lines. Why? Sometimes, they even go to different schools. Girls have been trained in sitting still and working quietly—that is why in the beginning they are generally better students (at least at rote learning) than boys, who are adventurous and active—and who have already developed healthy egos that require showing off and demanding attention.

While girls play with doll houses and paints (they paint pictures of more dolls and houses), boys build tall structures with blocks or speed down imaginary highways with cars and trucks—out, out into the world.

In the playground, girls skip rope and play jacks, while boys learn how to throw a ball and bat it and catch it, running, developing their bodies. Girls and boys often are separated for gym classes, even when they are six years old.

Play in school and at home is reinforced by the ads on television. Girls are shown with dolls that have dozens of dresses the manufacturer wants you to buy. You begin to think that having a lot of clothes must be the most important thing in a girl's life.

Boys on television are shown with trains and cars and chemistry sets, exciting games that take them into the world of adult work. Boys are not expected to be concerned mainly with what they wear.

In books, too, girls play quietly with dolls while boys fly kites, climb trees, explore caves, and make discoveries. It is not very surprising that there are few women scientists and engineers—girls are not supposed to be interested in how things grow, live, and work. Boys catch frogs, boys take apart old toasters and toy cars, and boys wonder about generating electricity and building bridges while girls wield toy brooms and dust mops.

Your school books tell you a lot about the roles of men and women. Girls grow up to be mommies, and their chief function is to take care of children and houses and to cook supper for daddies. Boys, on the other hand, go out to work. They are doctors and lawyers and businessmen. If girls work, they are nurses and secretaries. (Daddy's secretary is a woman.)

In one reader series used in California schools, a little girl falls down while she is trying on new skates. Her brother comments acidly, "Look at her, Mother. Just look at her. She is just like a girl. She gives up."

In other stories in the series, the boy in the family is seen playing with a rocket and toy space outfit while his sister is surrounded by dolls and plastic dishes.

One mother recalled an incident that occurred while she was reading to her daughter. She had just finished a line that said, "Architects, engineers, builders, and bankers put their heads together and work out plans."

"Why are there no ladies?" asked the little girl. The mother looked hastily: "Oh, yes, there's one," she said, and pointed to a secretary sitting at a table. And she explained to her daughter that there were women in all of the fields that had been mentioned but that most children's books just did not talk about them.

In another book, children were told to match workers with the tools of their trade. There was one woman in the group—and her "tool" was a shopping cart!

In stories about community life, men are the chairmen and officers; women take the minutes or serve the coffee and cake.

The lesson is not lost on young readers.

In school, too, you notice that most teachers are women but most principals are men. Bosses, you discover, are almost always men. The school doctor is a man; the school nurse is a woman. You don't even ask questions about that.

As you get to be seven and eight and nine, the roles of boys and girls are well set in your mind. Girls do not get dirty, do not fight, do not disobey orders, do not stay out past suppertime, do not cause trouble. Boys are lively youngsters with minds of their own, always getting into mischief, always trying to exert their own will against somebody else's, always experimenting, always daring, always investigating. And if they do not act properly as little girls do, well, "Boys will be boys." (Girls who do the same things are "horrid little tomboys.")

"Tomboy?" What is a tomboy? A girl who likes sports? Who feels free and more comfortable playing in blue jeans and sneakers than in prim organdy dresses and patent-leather shoes? Who would rather catch a fly ball than push a miniature baby carriage? Who wants to run and jump and engage in healthy, outdoor sports rather than make multicolored pot holders or embroider dish towels?

Teachers and parents cooperate in forcing girls and boys into the standard molds. "That's not a nice thing for a little girl to do." "That's not ladylike." "Girls are (or are not) supposed to do that." You fill in the blanks.

Boys are told to act like young men. Sometimes that means they ought to hit back when someone hits them and not run away. Often it means that they have to be good at sports. Boys who do not like sports and run away from fights are "sissies." Why? Boys suffer as much as girls from the roles they are taught while they are growing up.

As you grow older and become ten, eleven, and twelve, the differences become more pronounced. Boys and girls have not played together for years. Games are "girls' games" or "boys' games," and woe to the person who likes the games assigned to the other sex.

Boys become more boisterous and active as they assert their independence and individuality; girls become more gentle and quiet as they show their willingness to accept and conform to the rules of "ladylike" conduct.

If you are a girl, did you ever want to do the things boys were supposed to do? What happened? Did your mother say it wasn't proper? Or were you so well schooled in "proper feminine behavior" that you kept your wishes to yourself?

If you are a boy, did you ever wish that you did not have to compete in sports or fight the toughest kid on the block? Did your father tell you he wanted you to be "tough" and "manly"? Did it ever hurt to have to live up to all those images of what everyone seems to think a boy is?

By the time you are a teen-ager the role-playing gets more serious. You become more aware that there is an opposite sex—and you learn that those sexes are as opposite as they can be. Girls and boys even tote their school books differently, with girls holding them in front with both arms, while boys carry them with one hand at their side. (Many boys say the girls' way is easier, but it would be unmanly to switch!)

In some places, boys ride bikes to school—but girls won't; it "just isn't done." Boys, dressed in sneakers and pants, play ball at lunchtime recess while the girls stand around and watch—and comb their hair. Girls and boys run in packs, assimilating the standards of masculinity and femininity set by the group. It is a time when they are undergoing physical changes that truly relate to masculinity and femininity or, more accurately, to maleness and femaleness, yet the artificial stereotypes make this time of life even more difficult than it ought to be.

This is a time when girls' bodies begin to change, but who says "femininity" is related to the size of a girl's breasts or when they begin to develop? It just is not so, but many girls suffer because they think it is. This is a time when some boys begin to grow beards, but who is to say that whether this happens earlier or later is related to a boy's "masculinity." It just is not so.

If one girl cannot be more of a girl than another, how can she be more "feminine"? If one boy cannot be more of a boy than another, how can he be more "masculine"? The answers should be obvious, but myths and misconceptions cause a lot of unnecessary unhappiness.

# CHAPTER FOUR SEXISM IN HIGH SCHOOL

While most schools in the United States are coeducational, the education of girls and boys is so different that sometimes it seems as if there were two school systems coexisting in one. First, of course, there are schools that are "sexegrated" outright. Girls who are sent to commercial high schools learn typing or hairdressing skills while boys are trained to be machinists, printers, electricians, and the like—all jobs with as much as four and five times more pay than traditional "women's work."

Often, in the same schools, there are separate courses for boys and girls, with technical and mechanical skills like electronics, machine shops, and carpentry labeled "male," and cooking, sewing, and child care marked "female." In a technological society where we are all dependent on complex machines and equipment both at work and at home, this puts women at a distinct disadvantage. It also strengthens the notion that technical work is "male" and housework is "female."

Finally, the most invidious kind of segregation exists in the system of tracking boys and girls into separate fields of study, ensuring that they strive for different goals, and preparing them for separate careers.

Schools even discriminate against girls in extracurricular sports. A complaint of discrimination was filed by a Syracuse, New York, schoolteacher who charged that only male coaches were paid for working in after-school sports. The Syracuse school system spent about $90,000 for boys' extracurricular athletics compared to $200 for girls!

One sixteen-year-old high school girl filed a complaint with the human rights commission of her city because she had been barred from the boys' tennis team. There was no girls' team at the school and she was an expert player. The coach and team members all wanted her on the team, but she was kept out by the official male-only rules of interscholastic sports.

The system perpetuates itself. When girls see science and math classes filled entirely with boys, and taught by men, it is easy for them to conclude that those are "masculine" interests. If they ignore the stereotypes and decide that they want to be physicists, engineers, or accountants, guidance counselors often nudge them firmly back onto the "proper" path: "Wouldn't you rather take a secretarial course or be a teacher? It would fit in so much better with marriage and a family!"

Of course, most boys will someday marry and become fathers, but no one tells *them* that choosing a rewarding career will "interfere" with their marriage or their family.

Many guidance counselors act as though a girl's career is temporary and unimportant, while a man's choice of work is the most important decision he may make in his life. And girls come to believe this.

A social studies teacher who has taught in junior high and high school said, "I've heard girls say they wanted to take auto mechanics, and the guidance counselors and the mothers threw fits and absolutely shamed those girls out of wanting to take those courses."

She said, "The same thing is true when you get up into the more sophisticated classes like advanced math. It's okay for a girl to take advanced French or English or social studies, but when you get into advanced chemistry or physics or calculus, well, it's just not expected or encouraged."

An English teacher in a commercial high school reported: "Girls are encouraged to go into secretarial fields, but boys take courses that prepare them for running their own businesses."

Somehow in school, girls get the impression that it is "unfeminine" to be too smart. Mothers tell daughters not to act too bright in front of boys or they won't get dates: "Make him *think* he's smarter, dear."

"I remember one girl who was an honor student in elementary school," recalled a social studies teacher. "Then she discovered boys and she wanted to be popular. Well, to be popular in that particular group meant that you had to fail, so this girl, who had the potential for a very good academic career, went completely on the skids, deliberately, in order to compete for boys.

"It's around the eighth and ninth grade that this kind of thing begins to occur," she says. "Girls don't like to answer in class; they don't volunteer very often. If you call on a girl, she'll much more likely give you a blank stare while boys will try to think of an answer or make one up. Often, even if girls know the answer, they giggle and act stupid. They're always putting themselves down.

"Smart girls may work to hide their abilities. They say they never studied, they talk about other things, they giggle. They always say, 'Oh, but I'm such an idiot. This is probably not right, but. . . .' Most of them don't raise their hands.

"Even if girls don't have trouble with math, they say they do. They think math is somehow for boys. And they usually think they did much worse on an exam than they did—they say they flunked—boys don't say that. And the girls who assert themselves look strange to the rest.

"There are some very bright girls with supreme confidence, but a lot of it depends on the home background. If they're very bright but their parents think they shouldn't be, they're very ambivalent about it, and don't know what to do with themselves.

"If a boy thinks he is particularly smart, there's no shutting him up, but if a girl thinks she's smart, that doesn't necessarily mean she's going to be lively and talk a lot."

She went on to say, "Boys seem to develop a stronger ego by high school. . . . They have more confidence in themselves and are surer about their own worth."

"The girls have to know that it is all right for them to be bright," echoed another teacher. "They have to know that it is all right for them to do things. A girl has to know that she can be chairman of a school committee. She has to know this at ten years old, so by the time she is twelve and thirteen, when the pressure of dating and fashion and looks comes on, it doesn't mean that her intellectuality has to be put aside. It has to be shown somewhere in the elementary school that we do have a choice of roles, that there is not just one role for us."

Yet, although girls are generally brighter than boys in elementary school, they begin to slide in junior high and high school, and even more serious, they firmly establish the belief that it is "unfeminine" to be successful in school. Suddenly, femininity is equated with failure, a strange phenomenon that will show up again in their later lives.

In junior and senior high school, girls begin to give up all leadership roles to boys. One mother recalled, "My daughter came home very shocked because she had been made head of a committee. I said, 'Why should you be shocked?' and she answered that she had beat out a boy."

"Do the girls run for president or vice-president of the school?" asked one teacher. "No, they don't. Most presidents of the student body are boys. Maybe the girls don't run because they think they're going to lose, but why are they going to lose, and why don't they take the chance anyway?

"They are the secretaries. They have learned this at twelve and thirteen years old; so, by the time they are mature, why shouldn't they think of themselves as secretaries? And why do they make good secretaries? Because they have had the training from the time they were twelve! They have been trained to serve men. Boys are the class officers and the editors of the papers and magazines. I don't think they are taking it away from the girls. I don't think the girls are even trying to get those jobs."

"In one seventh-grade class we wrote our own constitution," said the social studies teacher. "Then we elected a government—and the president was a boy, the senators were boys—one or two of the representatives were girls—but all the higher officers were boys. One of the girls typed it up! And this was a very bright class.

"In history club," she added, "the higher officers are generally boys and the secretaries are girls. And when they run for class office, the boys are elected to high positions, and the girls are secretaries again."

One teacher admitted that sometimes teachers take advantage of the brainwashing that has occurred. "The girls are our helpers, our little secretaries," she said. "They help with the roll, they mark papers for you, they get coffee—all the menial tasks. The only thing the boys will help you with is moving things. They'll pull the map down. Sometimes I send the girls down for books, so they know they have physical strength too."

Girls have few role models to look up to in school. "Men are always the chairmen of departments, and the kids know it," said one teacher. "Women are not in positions of authority in the school system. In my school there are two women chairmen—I'll give you a guess which. Home economics and library. There are no women chairmen in any of the academic departments of my school, and I have met only two women department chairmen in this whole county. I don't know any women principals or assistant principals outside elementary school and no women superintendents of schools. If girls could see women in positions of authority in the school system, they would have a stronger idea of what a woman can do."

She recalled an article in the school paper written by a boy about the new president of the school board. "His first sentence was, 'Why would a woman want to be president of the school board?' If it were a man, he never would have said that. The girls and boys see this; they see what's going on."

Often the guidance counselors themselves discourage bright, ambitious girls. First, they give them brochures which always seem to refer to a secretary or a nurse as "she." Then they ask girls whether the careers they have in mind would "fit in" with marriage and a family, whether they will find opportunities in other parts of the country if their husbands' jobs take them to other cities. Nobody asks boys the same questions or assumes that they should make such adjustments for their wives.

Girls come to believe, therefore, that their most important role in life is marrying and bearing children. If they think about working, they seldom think far beyond being airline stewardesses, beauticians, nurses, teachers, or secretaries.

Teachers add to the role problem by not expecting girls to do as well in "male" fields like science and math. It has been proven that students' success in school is partly dependent on the teachers' expectations; and a school that restricts drafting and machine-shop courses to boys is not a good influence for a girl trying to decide whether or not she might become an engineer.

Parents discourage girls too, by talking to sons about *their* futures as doctors, lawyers, and engineers, but filling girls full of the prospect of motherhood—as if that was all they ought to look forward to. Career aspirations are not expected, and if they do exist, they are seldom taken seriously.

A girl begins thinking about her future at the same time that her sex-role identity is being established—and at a time when she is especially sensitive to the attitudes of her friends and classmates, all of whom have been taught to believe that marriage and motherhood are a woman's chief purpose. As a result, boys and girls accept the stereotyped notion that a girl with a strong career drive is "unfeminine," and, as a result of this, in later life men may feel their egos threatened by competition from women workers or by the desire of their own wives to work. It becomes a vicious cycle.

As a result of all this brainwashing, many women think very little of their own ability, lack confidence, feel that it is a waste of time to be ambitious, and think that working for a successful career will conflict with their personal happiness.

Even if girls do go to college, they put their careers second to marriage. Some girls joke about going to college to get their "M.R.S.," and "Although a girl has had high ambitions," said one teacher, "if she meets a boy, then everything changes. If she meets a guy who wants to be a doctor, she will forget about her career and go to work to put him through school. His education still comes first."

What, then, do young women do? Many work at "feminine"—meaning low-paid, low-status—jobs, while they live with the belief that the only socially approved way to find their own personal identity and self-expression is to marry a man and produce children.

If anthropologists a thousand years from now were to study the practice of "dating," they might consider it one of the most bizarre customs they had ever seen—one that was calculated to make young boys and girls suffer terrible pain while they pretended to enjoy themselves.

Dating is the first instance where the male/female roles devised by society cause almost universal discontent. Boys and girls are extremely insecure at this age. They are unsure of themselves; they are often unable to communicate their feelings to others, especially to those of the opposite sex, and they are extremely sensitive to slights and rejections.

So, what does the dating system do? It forces boys to make all the advances—whether the individual boy is aggressive or shy—and it requires girls to hint or flirt or sit quietly by, waiting anxiously for some boy to take the lead. Increasingly, boys and girls are speaking up to say the system is harmful to everyone and just does not make sense.

One of the ill effects is the competition it fosters among girls. "The girls are really bad to each other," says a teacher. "They make the boys the prize. They are catty, they put each other down, they drop friends. They try to outdo each other with clothes and makeup. It causes a lot of unhappiness."

After years of forced separation at play, boys and girls are suddenly brought together. But, now they find they have not learned how to be ordinary friends. They have to be boyfriend and girl friend. They are uncomfortable and nervous talking to each other. They have to abide by strict social rules—they cannot be "just good friends." Of course some can, but they are the exceptions. Girls as well as boys have been brought up to believe that the other sex is so strange and different that no wonder they find it hard to relate to each other simply as human beings.

On the one hand, girls, who have been brought up to be wives and mothers, start thinking of their boyfriends as future husbands and scribble their names with "Mrs." in front of them, and on the other, the boys imitate the standards of our culture that rate women by how they look. And they have had so little experience in relating to girls in a personal way that they can only think in terms of the games and conquests of sex.

The rules about who pays on dates also cause discomfort and dissatisfaction. "I always feel like I'm being rented for the evening," says one girl, only half joking. "I have to be nice and charming and do what he wants to do because he's paying."

Boys do not like the system either. After all, teen-age boys do not have any more money than teen-age girls, and it is often a burden for them to pay for two. Yet, girls do not volunteer to pay their share because they think it would hurt the boy's ego, and boys do not ask the girls to go "Dutch" for fear of insulting them. Teen-agers talk to each other a lot, but they often do not say the things that are really on their minds.

The dating system is tied to the myths of femininity and masculinity—that women ought to be passive and men ought to be aggressive. The practice of men paying for women goes back to the time when women did not work outside the home and had no incomes—or if they did work, they earned so little money that they could not afford to pay for entertainment. Although most women still earn less money than men, some find that they enjoy dates more when they pay their own way. And it is easier to ask a man (or a boy) out, if you are not asking him to spend money on you.

Social patterns do not change overnight, and it is possible—even likely—that the next generation will face the same anguish about dating that teen-agers face now. It is, however, an issue that has been raised by the feminist movement and one worth thinking about.

1900181

# CHAPTER FIVE BARRIERS IN HIGHER EDUCATION

Suppose you are a young woman who is going to graduate from high school soon, and in spite of all the myths you have learned about a woman's "true role," nobody has asked you to marry him yet. So, you will just have to go off to college or out to work. Maybe that is even what you want to do!

Did you know that more girls finish high school than boys—and that they win a higher percentage of high school honors? Nevertheless, a smaller percentage of girls enter college than men. Women now make up only 40 percent of the undergraduate college population. Colleges often have quotas that work against women students, and this is not against the law. (Legislation has been introduced in Congress to change this.)

At the University of North Carolina, for example, the admission of freshman women is "restricted to those who are especially well qualified." There is no such restriction for men.

A study of educational facilities in Virginia, released in 1964, reported that during a period of time in which 21,000 women were turned down for college admission, not one man was rejected.

An admissions officer at the University of Michigan admitted accepting boys who had test scores, high school grades, and recommendations inferior to those of girls who were turned down.

Some admissions officers say openly, "What does a woman need a degree for—to be a wife and mother? They're just going to get married and all this education will have been wasted."

It is worse in graduate and professional schools. At the University of California Law School recently, there were 5 women out of 340 students. There were 250 men and no women enrolled in the university's medical school.

Even if girls are admitted to the traditional "male-only" haunts, they are not made especially welcome. One young woman was not assigned a locker for her laboratory class in the school of engineering she was attending. After being shunted from one staff member to another, she was informed that the lockers were in the men's bathroom —she could have one if she wanted it there.

That same university declared that it admitted very few women to its medical school and that it had no intention of increasing the number, because "women get married and do not continue in the profession." Across the country, the percentage of medical degrees awarded women has not increased since 1920; women still only comprise 7 percent (about 20,000) of the doctors in this country.

Even if women win admission to college and graduate schools, they face discrimination when scholarships and fellowships are awarded. At Columbia University, for example, fellowships are given to men, unmarried women, married women, and married women with children—in that order. One professor who was questioned about this practice retorted that women didn't need Ph.D.'s to be good wives and mothers.

In spite of all the prejudice against women in colleges and graduate schools, the real facts are that women are more successful in school than men—68 percent of women undergraduates have averages of B or better, compared to 54 percent of the men. And a study done at the University of Michigan showed that 76.5 percent of the women who entered in 1965 graduated in 1969, compared to only 60.8 percent of the men.

It is even more difficult for women in graduate school, where only 36 percent of the masters' candidates and 13 percent of the doctoral candidates are women. These low figures are due in part to the familiar pattern of women dropping out of school when they marry so they can work to help their husbands complete their educations or so they can take care of the babies they bear.

In school, women are concentrated in those traditional "female fields" again. One out of three college women majors in education. However, that may have to change. The government has warned that the teaching shortage is just about over. Now, women will find it hard to get jobs even in education.

Women who do not choose teaching generally stick to areas like English, the arts, foreign languages, and literature. Some go into practically all-female fields like home economics, early-childhood education, nursing, library science, and occupational and physical therapy. Only 6 percent choose economics and fewer pick business and commerce.

It is hard to know how much a girl's choices are influenced by stereotype and tradition and how much by outright discrimination. For example, women receive under 5 percent of the professional degrees in fields like law, architecture, and engineering.

Only 2 percent of the engineers in the United States are women compared to about 33 percent in Europe. Yet tests have shown that 40 percent of those with an aptitude for engineering are women. Unfortunately, if a girl does not think engineering is labeled "male," chances are that the admissions officer at the engineering school does.

In college, a girl makes decisions about work and the future that are among the most important in her life. Everyone admits the importance of "role models" in making those choices, yet, there again, women do not find many more models than they did in high school.

Only 22 percent of college teachers are women—and that is a smaller ratio than in 1930. Most of them are in the lower categories, working as instructors and assistant professors, while men hold the high-paid prestigious jobs as professors, department chairman, and the like. Women college presidents are a rarity—even in all-girl colleges.

If and when girls do get to college, they swiftly find out that a "woman's place" is not in academia. The University of Chicago, for example, has a lower percentage of women on its faculty now than it did in 1899. A study of 188 sociology departments across the country showed that women are 30 percent of doctoral candidates but only 4 percent of full professors. At Columbia University, 25 percent of the doctorates go to women students, but only 2 percent of tenured faculty members are women, and they are only 5.2 percent of full professors—including Barnard, the associated women's college, where only 22 percent of full professors are women. A recent survey at the University of Pennsylvania showed that there were twenty-six departments with no women faculty members at all.

The few women chairmen in colleges and universities are usually in departments of education and home economics: finding any women teachers in math and physics departments is unusual. Teaching may be a "woman's field," but that holds true only for elementary and secondary schools, where the pay and prestige are lowest, and where the students are children who, according to our stereotypes, ought to be cared for by women.

It is not surprising then that women are discouraged from pursuing academic careers. The percentage of women who receive bachelors, masters, and doctoral degrees has actually *decreased* since 1930. (Women have held their share in the number of bachelors' and professional degrees [40 percent] but have fallen from over 40 to 35 percent of masters' and from over 15 to under 12 percent of Ph.D.'s.)

For years women college students have been fighting another kind of discrimination on campus—perhaps not as serious as academic discrimination, but annoying and insulting in its own way. College women often are forced to adhere to social regulations that do not apply to men. They are bound by curfew requirements to sign in and out as well as by rules that apply to out-of-town visits. Even though women students are old enough to get married, many colleges think they must tell them when to go to bed.

At Elmira College in New York, girls protested a rule that forced them to sign out and to be back by midnight. There was no such regulation for boys. Some colleges have done away with these rules, but others still treat women as if they were children.

In small ways like this, and in larger ways like strict quota systems, colleges tell women that they are different from men—and in fact, that they are not as good as men in many fields—that they just do not belong. Small wonder that actual experiments have shown that women have come to believe that they are inferior. The culture of sexism is an effective brainwasher.

# CHAPTER SIX WOMEN GET THE WORST WORK

Imagine you have been successful in getting into college, and now you are out. Or you have finished high school and are starting to look for a job. And don't say, "I'm not going to work, I'm going to get married." That is a myth that belongs more in the movies than in real life. First of all, one out of every ten women does not get married, and secondly, nine out of ten women will work at some time in their lives even if they do get married.

A girl born in 1900 could expect to live about forty-eight years; now that life expectancy has increased to seventy-four. If a woman marries in her twenties and has her children by the time she is thirty, she will be sending them off to school when she is thirty-five—and that leaves nearly forty years of life that is no longer limited by a young child's constant dependency. Even if she wishes (and can afford) to stay home until the children are teen-agers (though half the mothers of school-age children work) that still leaves some thirty years to fill.

Since, whether a woman marries and raises children or not, she is probably going to work for anywhere from twenty-five to forty-five years, it is only prudent to take a look at the work world out there and see what it holds in store for women. Here is one indicator.

The Barnard College placement service reports that the airlines want college *men* for management and college *women* for stewardesses and secretaries. One publishing company called the service about a trainee program. The company promised to prepare the women to be editors—but first they had to know shorthand and typing!

That is not unusual. About one out of every five women with *four years of college* ends up in clerical, sales, service, or semi-skilled factory jobs.

What about girls who go to work straight from high school? Six out of ten get clerical jobs and another 25 percent are service or factory workers. For dropouts, it is even worse—four out of ten become service and household domestic workers, 33 percent get factory jobs, and a minority are hired as clerks.

Generally, the rule of thumb is this: when male high school or college graduates go on job interviews they are given aptitude tests; females are given typing tests. Some people warn women college graduates never to admit they can type, or they will find themselves in dead-end secretarial work.

The picture is pretty dim. Today, women are still forced into the lowest-paying, least desirable jobs with little chance of advancement. Even when they do the same work as men, they often receive less pay. Many kinds of jobs are simply marked "off limits" to women, while others are shunned by men as "beneath them." Which sex do you think of when you say "business executive"? Which sex when you say "secretary"? Women are 97 percent of secretaries and only 2 percent of management personnel. Why can it not be the other way around?

"But they do not really need the money," or "They are just going to get married and quit," say a lot of men—and even some women. The facts are that 49 percent of the women in this country work (including 57 percent of all black women); that over 40 percent (12.3 million) of these women are single, widowed, divorced, or separated (Who says they really do not need the money?); and that 17.6 million are married (Who says that when women get married they quit their jobs?).

Women are 38 percent of the nation's work force—and they work for the same reasons as men. Most work for the money, some because it gives them satisfaction and fulfillment. However, they do not earn 38 percent of the money paid out in the nation's salaries—not by a long shot. On the average, women earn fifty-eight cents for every dollar that men earn. This gap exists in every area of work—from clerical to professional—and on the whole, the difference has gotten greater over the last fifteen years. A woman with a college degree earns an average of $6,694 per year, barely more than a man with an eighth-grade education, who earns $6,580. A male college graduate is paid $11,795.

Women clerical workers earned approximately $4,789 in 1968 compared to $7,351 for men. Women professional and technical workers received $6,691 compared to $10,151 for men. Service workers were paid $3,332 compared to $6,058 for men, and saleswomen received $3,461 compared to $8,549 for salesmen.

Many times, men working in department stores, for example, will be put in departments where they can earn high commissions, while women working the same hours in the same stores come home with half as much in their pay envelopes. This pay gap applies to factory workers as well as to managers and administrators.

The Equal Pay Act, which in 1963 made it illegal to pay women less than men for the same jobs, has resulted in at least $2 million in back pay to women workers. The administrator of the federal program said that in 1970 another $17 million was due thousands of women. It was also in 1970 that $250,000 was awarded to 230 women packers of glass containers at the Wheaton Glass Company in Millville, New Jersey, because they were paid two and a half cents less per hour than men even though they did the same work. As a result of that case, a Federal Appeals Court ruled in favor of women workers at the American Can Company's Dixie Products Division in Fort Smith, Arkansas. The Federal Wage and Hour Administration had charged that the women working as cup machine operators were being underpaid twenty cents an hour, and it demanded $100,000 in back wages.

Most companies do not appear willing to obey the law on their own, and the government only has enough staff in its Wage and Labor Standard Administration to enforce it in a minimal way. Furthermore, the Equal Pay Act does not apply at all to women in professional, executive, or administrative jobs. (In fact, it excludes half the jobs in America.)

The expected monthly salaries for June, 1970, college graduates showed the need for the act's extension. They included: in liberal arts $631 for women, $688 for men; in engineering $844 for women, $872 for men; in economics and finance $700 for women, $718 for men; in accounting $746 for women, $832 for men; and in chemistry $765 for women, $806 for men; and the gap widens as the men get raises and the women are left behind.

One woman engineer, for example, graduated from a prominent Eastern university and left several jobs after she was denied promotions in each. At that point she had so much trouble getting *any* job, that after a year she settled for a position as assistant to a quality control engineer at $150 a week. Her boss said, "We thought she couldn't be good if she was willing to work for that kind of money, but we didn't want to spend more. However, she is qualified to do much better than this."

One of the reasons women earn less than men is that they are simply excluded from whole categories of work—the most lucrative ones. Over 64 percent of women workers are in clerical, service, sales, or domestic work while 70 percent of men are professional and technical workers, managers, owners, craftsmen, foremen, or skilled factory workers—all jobs that pay more and promise advancement. In 1968, over 33 percent of women workers had clerical jobs, 16 percent were service workers, 15 percent factory workers, and 15 percent professional and technical workers (66 percent of those were teachers or nurses).

Did you ever notice how most restaurants have either waiters or waitresses, but not both? Somehow, the expensive restaurants, where tips are high, have waiters. Waitresses work mostly in luncheonettes and moderate-priced restaurants. A group of waitresses in New York City filed a complaint against a restaurant owner who fired them all because he decided he wanted men for the job. *Think about all this the next time you go out to eat.*

The story among United States government workers is just as bad. While one-third of federal employees are women, they are concentrated in the lowest clerical jobs. They are only 6.9 percent of workers who earn $15,000 and above, and hold only about 1.5 percent of the posts that pay $25,000 and above. Even though it is no longer legal to specifically request men for the highest jobs, somehow women are conspicuous by their absence.

In technical areas, women are usually in the lowest categories—like draftsman or engineering technician. If they work in factories, they are rarely foremen, and they are assigned the least rewarding jobs—often with the excuse of hours, or weight-lifting limitations. (The weight-lifting requirements are sometimes added to the job so that women can be excluded. However, recent court decisions are expected to invalidate these restrictions.)

One of the most impenetrable bastions of male supremacy is the world of management.

*"Open the ranks to women in banks!*
*It's a shocker—no women at Crocker.*
*Employment without promotion is slavery.*
*Crocker Execs are all of one sex.*
*The Board of Directors are women rejectors!"*

That was the chant heard when a group of San Francisco women picketed the Crocker Citizens' National Bank in July, 1970, charging that while it employed six thousand women (65 percent of the total staff), no women had ever been officers or had any of the bank's top-paying jobs, that only five women were counted in any of the top five hundred posts, and only 4 percent of even the lowest level supervisory positions were held by women.

The American Society for Personnel Administration did a survey in 1970 and found that almost 60 percent of the companies that responded refused to hire women for some jobs. Almost 75 percent of them had under 5 percent women in professional and technical jobs. Some 87 percent had 5 percent or fewer women in middle management and above. A survey of 366 companies in Cleveland, Ohio, revealed that 90 percent of them believed that women should only be hired in secretarial, clerical, and bookkeeping jobs—this, in spite of the fact that 20 percent of college-age women are graduating from college today, and there are nearly 3 million women with college degrees in the United States.

As a tragic result, many women find themselves in jobs far below their talents and training. One-third of all women workers are in only seven occupations: secretary, retail store saleswoman, household worker, elementary school teacher, bookkeeper, waitress, nurse.

Unfortunately, women do not get discounts in stores or movie houses or on buses. They do not get a 42 percent discount on rent or groceries because they earn that much less money. They are just more likely than men to be poor. Some 20 percent of women workers receive under $3,000 a year compared to 8 percent for men. About 60 percent of women workers earn under $5,000 a year compared to 20 percent of all men. And only 3 percent of women earn over $10,000 compared to 28 percent of men.

Almost 50 percent of all minority women workers are in service work, with half of them working in private households. Private household workers (maids, in plain language) earn an average of $1,523 for working full time all year. And they are excluded from the right to unemployment insurance and workmen's compensation. Though they are covered by social security, employers often fail to report their earnings to avoid paying the tax.

Women also are hit the hardest by unemployment, with a rate almost twice that of men. Half the jobless people in the country are women, though women are only 38 percent of the work force. The rate is worse for teen-age girls, with unemployment 12.1 percent for white girls and 28.8 percent for black girls compared to 11.6 percent for white boys and 22.1 percent for black boys.

The fact that women earn less—either because they are forced into the least desirable jobs, are paid less for equal work, or are faced with greater unemployment—results in the fact that there are more poverty-stricken women than men (11.2 million women over the age of sixteen in 1966) compared with 6.9 million men). And families where the only wage earner is a woman are two or three times as likely to be poor as those where a man is working (in 40 percent of all marriages the wife also works). Over one out of ten American families are supported only by women. And 33 percent of those 5.4 million families live in poverty.

It is worse for minority groups. About 62 percent of the minority families with only women wage earners are poor (3.8 million poor people) compared to 30 percent for whites (3.6 million poor people). And one out of every four black families has only a woman to support it; those families account for over half the poor blacks in America.

One analyst figured out that a child living in a poor family with a male wage earner had a fifty-fifty chance of making it out of poverty from 1960 to 1970. In those years, the number of poor families supported by men fell from 5 million to 2.5 million. However, that child had no chance at all if his or her family was supported by a woman.

Even when a family has a father and mother living together, a woman's wages are hardly superfluous. (Who ever decided that a husband's wages are "what counts" and the wife's salary is "only helping"? They may use one paycheck for the rent and the other for groceries. Which one is "helping"?)

Almost 5 million women workers have husbands who earn under $5,000 a year. Half of all working wives have husbands who earn under $7,000 a year, still far below the $9,197 income for a family of four which the government says is necessary for a moderate standard of living. And 40 percent of working wives account for over 33 percent of their family's income. They would account for more if they did not suffer job and salary discrimination.

A Gallup Poll in 1969 found that two out of three husbands want their wives to work. Families with working wives have higher standards of living—30 percent higher than for families where only the husband works.

Of course, there are large numbers of women who are not married. More than a fifth of women workers are single (6.5 million) and almost an equal number are widowed, divorced, or separated (5.8 million). In fact, that myth about divorced women lying on chaise lounges munching on chocolates and living off alimony is just that—a myth. About 72 percent of divorced women work, and many of those that do not are unable to because they have small children and no child-care facilities (1.5 million divorced women are taking care of children) or they are elderly.

There are many myths about women workers used by employers to rationalize discrimination. They say that women have higher absentee rates than men, and that they are more likely to leave their jobs. This is untrue. According to the Labor Department, a worker's absentee rate and turnover rate is directly related not to sex, but to whether he or she is in a good job with advancement or whether it is a badly paying deadend job. In fact, supervisors at a Republic Steel plant in South Chicago said that absenteeism is a never-ending problem with men workers, but it was no problem at all with the women who recently had been hired. And, they added, the women also came to work on time. There is little absenteeism or turnover among executives of either sex, the government points out.

Statistics concerning illness and disability also disprove some of the common stereotypes. Women lose more time from acute illness, but men lose more work days from chronic diseases like heart trouble and arthritis. Women's illnesses keep them away from work for shorter periods than men, so that men lose more time from disability than do women—including the time women take off for pregnancy and childbirth. The government has figured that the total financial loss for male and female absences is about the same. Since women, on the average, live seven years longer than men and are not as subject to heart disease (the nation's number one killer) that afflicts so many men after they pass forty, it could even be argued that women are *better* risks for the top jobs in government and industry.

More than ever before, women are beginning to challenge the old bastions of male supremacy in the work world. They are taking jobs of every description, from stockbroker to aquanaut.

Five scientists, in July, 1970, were the first women aquanauts in the government's underwater research program in the Virgin Islands. They reported a good deal of male chauvinism from the men they worked with. "They were protective to the point of harassment," said Dr. Sylvia Mead, a botanist. "They kept saying, sort of sarcastically, that they didn't want us to hurt ourselves." She added that "the only thing men could do down there that we couldn't do was grow beards." Far away, in another part of the globe, four women from The Ohio State University Polar Studies program in 1969 became the first women scientists to conduct research in Antarctica.

Women are also beginning to move into executive spots in business. In 1965, Phyllis Peterson and Julia Walsh were admitted to the American Stock Exchange and became the first women members of a major exchange in this country. The New York Stock Exchange, which did not even allow women on the trading floor, finally admitted a female to its membership in 1967, when Muriel Siebert was accepted to a roster that included 1,364 men. A second woman, Jane Larkin, was admitted in 1970.

Women are moving into technical jobs. In Wilburton, Oklahoma, Linda Little, who is in her twenties, climbs telephone poles in her job as a lineman with the Oklahoma Western Telephone Company. In New York City, Danis Cascio is an engineering student who has worked as an inspector on street and sewer construction jobs.

Ann Hutchinson is another kind of engineer. At only thirty-one, she helped develop the vidicon television tube that permitted detailed pictures of the surface of Mars to be relayed to earth. Another woman, Laurel van der Wal, sent mice into space as part of important experiments in biochemical space engineering.

One huge area of employment that has traditionally been closed to women is the crafts that require apprenticeship training—machinist, electrician, sheet-metal worker, carpenter, pipefitter. In 1968, less than 1 percent of the 278,000 apprentices in the United States were women, and they were limited to low-paying "women's" jobs like beautician, dressmaker, and dental technician.

However, there has been an increase of women in these fields. Some 1,800 women in 1969 were learning to be plumbers, aircraft and auto mechanics, construction workers, cheesemakers, shoe repairmen, watchmakers, laboratory technicians, and other skilled craftsmen. The Women's Bureau of the Labor Department gives examples of the upsurge—a woman who is an apprentice gyro repairer at Robins Air Force Base in Georgia; an airborne electronic-computer repair apprentice in Oklahoma; a woman who is learning to be a cameraman, stripper, and platemaker at a lithograph company in Washington, D.C. And they will earn twice and three times the salaries they would have been paid as clerks or secretaries.

"How could a jury believe a woman? How could a woman stand the 'blue' language of the weekly staff meetings? How could she get along with FBI agents?" These were some of the incredible questions asked Shirah Neiman, a magna cum laude graduate of Columbia Law School, when she applied for a job as Assistant United States Attorney in the office that handles all federal prosecutions in New York City. A group of women law students were prepared to file a suit charging sex discrimination because the United States Attorney's office had not hired a woman criminal lawyer in twenty years, and it was common knowledge that it did not want any. Finally, in September, 1970, Shirah Neiman got the job.

In another area of law, women were not so lucky. The University of Michigan Law School faculty voted unanimously to bar the law firm of Royall, Koegel, Rogers, and Wells from using the university's recruiting facilities. A company recruiter had told students that the firm would hire fewer women than men and that those women would need higher qualifications. William Rogers belonged to that law firm before he became President Nixon's Secretary of State.

The percentage of women lawyers has actually decreased since 1950. In that year one out of every twenty-eight lawyers was a woman, but in 1967 only one out of forty was a woman. Only a handful are partners in major firms. Yet this may change in the future. Increasing numbers of women are studying law. As an example, consider Radcliffe College, where half the 1970 graduates applied for admission to law school.

Advances have been made in some unconventional occupations. Jean Brady, forty-seven, in 1970 became the first woman dealer at a Las Vegas gambling house—a job that pays about sixty-five dollars a day in salary and tips. Women had been barred from those jobs for thirty years. A representative of one casino gave the excuse that, "We have a lot of Mormons in Las Vegas, and what with that and the general Puritan ethic about it, we have never hired women as dealers at the tables." Somehow, the Puritan ethic did not prevent them from hiring women as scantily clad waitresses or topless dancers. "Well, that's different," asserted the casino spokesman. He did not explain how or why.

Some corporations appear to be looking for more women in management—or so they say. And at the Columbia University School of Business, there were seventy women students in 1970 compared to twenty women three years before. Women will be demanding management jobs, whether business is ready or not.

# CHAPTER SEVEN
# WHO CARES FOR THE CHILDREN?

One of the favorite arguments against hiring women for responsible positions is that they will marry, get pregnant, and leave. The fact is that 10.6 million women (38 percent of all women workers) are mothers with children under eighteen—and some 4.2 million of them have children under six. Over 25 percent of mothers with children under three work, 37 percent of women with children from three to five work, and more than 50 percent of all women with children six to seventeen work. The conclusion can be drawn that mothers are twice as likely to work when their children are in school and do not require day-long care. The problem within the United States is that there are only meager child-care facilities for the millions of children whose mothers want to work.

There are places in day-care centers (some are also open at night) for only about half a million children in this country, while the number of young children of mothers already working is estimated at more than ten times that figure. There are also few after-school programs to care for primary-school children too young to be left alone.

As a result, the children of working mothers are cared for by relatives, friends, older brothers and sisters, or by the woman herself on the job. And some of them become "latchkey kids," with keys around their necks and instructions to take care of themselves.

During World War II, when it was considered "patriotic" for women to work in defense plants, there were spaces in day-care centers for six times as many children as now. Most of those facilities were closed after the war ended.

For many working mothers, their jobs are hardly unnecessary "diversions" to bring in extra spending money, though they would have just as much right to work if they were. Of all working mothers with children under six, one in three are either divorced, separated, widowed (50 percent of those mothers work), or have husbands who earn under $5,000.

Child care is not a serious problem for the rich who can afford private housekeepers or expensive nursery schools. However, even middle-class women cannot afford private child-care centers that charge as much as $2,500 a year; and with the taxes and the carfare, the clothing and the lunch expenses involved in any job, it hardly pays a woman to hire a full-time babysitter: she would be paying out her entire salary.

Although a businessman can deduct expensive lunches with clients as part of his necessary business expenses, a working mother cannot deduct the child-care expenses that make it possible for her to work at all. (The existing law allows a $600 deduction for one child and $900 for two or more in families where the *joint* income is not above $6,900—hardly a great boon to most people. There is no such limit on business lunches.)

Federal and state legislation provide money for the construction and staffing of a limited number of child-care centers that are restricted to the poor. The philosophy behind those laws has been that child care is needed so that women on welfare can work and save the state money—not that *all* parents have a right to government-supported child care. And the amount of money appropriated is not nearly sufficient to establish child-care facilities even for the poor.

A study by the Department of Health, Education, and Welfare revealed that in 1969, nearly one out of every six welfare mothers who was working or enrolled in a job training program left her children to take care of themselves while she was away from home.

Some companies and unions have set up child-care centers for their own workers. Generally parents pay for this service on a sliding scale and the company covers the rest. The Skyland Textile Company in Morgantown, North Carolina; KLH, which manufactures stereophonograph systems and other high-fidelity equipment in Cambridge, Massachusetts; and the Amalgamated Clothing Workers in Chicago have all set up centers for their workers' children—and sometimes for the children of other people in the community. It has been found that the establishment of such facilities cuts down absenteeism and generally improves the morale of women workers who are confident that their children are being well cared for.

Nearly one hundred hospitals have set up child-care centers (some running for twenty-four hours) for the children of nurses and other employees. Some universities provide facilities for the children of their students and faculty—and women's groups are pressing more universities to do the same.

It is estimated that it costs about $200,000 to set up a child-care center, with operating costs that run $2,000 per child each year. However, some mothers have ignored these estimates and have set up cooperative child-care arrangements in vacant stores. One group that established a program in New York sent out a plea for "toys, nonperishable foods, tables and chairs, paints and brushes, hammers, saws, nails, children's scissors—the other kind, too—glue, paper, and does anyone have an extra refrigerator, hot plate, or record player?" They completely redecorated two adjoining stores and welcomed all the parents in the neighborhood to join in the venture. Men as well as women staff the program so that the boys and girls do not grow up to believe that caring for children is exclusively a woman's role.

The demand for free, twenty-four-hour child care to be available to all economic groups is a key demand of the feminist movement. Twenty-four-hour care means that the centers will be open at all times to care for children of parents who work evenings, nights, or weekends, not that parents are expected to put their children in centers and never return. A July, 1969, Gallup Poll showed that two-thirds of the American public favor the establishment of child-care centers supported by the Federal government.

# CHAPTER EIGHT
# AGAINST COMPULSORY PREGNANCY

Another key feminist issue also related to a woman's role as a mother is abortion. Many normal pregnancies naturally end in abortions—they are called miscarriages. Feminists, however, are talking about "induced abortion." Although it has been used as a means of birth control in 99 percent of all the societies studied by anthropologists, in most of the fifty states of America, abortion is still illegal except when it is performed to save the mother's life.

Abortion was not illegal in the United States until 1821, when Connecticut became the first state to pass a law to ban it. Until 1869, even Catholics were not opposed to early abortions aimed at saving a mother's life. Then church doctrine changed, theologians promoted the belief that the soul enters the body at conception rather than at "quickening" (when the fetus begins to move), and Pope Pius IX issued a declaration that abortion was murder.

By 1970, abortion was legal for all reasons in only three states—New York, Hawaii, and Alaska. New York alone does not have a residence requirement.

Since 1967, laws have been changed in about a dozen other states to allow abortion to protect a woman's physical or mental health, in the event of rape or incest, or if the infant would be born deformed. However, such conditions affect only a small minority of the women who want abortions. Most of them (the majority are married) just do not want another child.

Every year, about one million illegal abortions are performed in the United States upon women who would rather pay the high prices of willing doctors or suffer the danger of treatment by people with no medical training than undergo a forced pregnancy. In the United States there is one abortion for every four births, but only 1 percent are legal—and most of those are for the rich. In fact, doctors say that nine out of ten abortions performed in private hospitals "stretch" the law—rich women have always been able to get abortions when they wanted them.

It is the lower and middle classes that suffer. About one thousand deaths a year result from bungled abortions—and countless other women are rushed to hospitals bleeding from a pierced uterus or other complications. Ironically, an abortion is a very simple operation. When it is performed by trained personnel, it is about *eight times safer than normal childbirth.* In England, where abortions are legal, the death rate from abortion is lower than from tonsilectomy.

Studies in Sweden have shown that it is not a very good idea to bring an unwanted child into the world. An investigation of Swedish children born as a result of governmental refusal to grant abortions showed that in later life these children were more likely to be arrested for drunkenness or criminal behavior, they received less education, and they needed more psychiatric care than did other children.

Some opponents of abortion argue that the fetus is a human life. Scientists say that it is merely a mass of cells—that life does not occur until the infant is born. Opponents also say that someone great may have been lost to the world by abortion. That is an argument also used against any kind of contraception (including rhythm). When you stop to think that most women are fertile for more than thirty years, the numbers of children women would have without the use of contraceptives or abortion are staggering.

They are especially staggering to people concerned with the population explosion. And overpopulation is related to the problem of ecology. More people means: more raw materials used, more garbage produced, more air-polluting power plants and automobiles required, and more river-polluting factories established to manufacture needed goods. This earth can hold just so many people comfortably.

In 6000 B.C., there were 5 million people on the earth. That number doubled once every thousand years until it reached 500 million in A.D. 1650. It doubled again to a billion in 1850, doubled once more to 2 billion in 1930 and is scheduled to double again by the year 2000. We already have more than 3 billion people on the earth and the doubling time is getting shorter.

The situation is most serious in underdeveloped countries where some 3.5 million people—mostly children—starve to death every year. The doubling time in Nigeria is 28 years, in Turkey 24 years, and in Brazil 22 years. Effective birth-control programs (in spite of all the opposition) have slowed things down to 63 years in the United States and Russia, 140 years in England, and 175 years in Austria.

One of the solutions is the plea within the United States for "zero population growth"; that is, the country should seek to maintain a constant population. Since we have cut the death rate and people are living longer, we will increase our population even if each couple has no more than two children.

The answer is not to put quotas on how many children a couple may have—though that has been suggested—but to make birth control and abortion easily available for all who want it.

A study done by the Princeton University Office of Population Research revealed that 35 to 45 percent of all the births in the United States in the past ten years have been unwanted by at least one of the parents responsible. A higher percentage of unwanted children plagued the poor—42 percent—compared to 17 percent among other economic groups. The study showed that there were about 2.7 million unwanted poor babies in the ten-year period, compared to about 3.2 million unwanted middle-class and rich babies. Some 62 percent of the women in the survey had had at least one unwanted pregnancy, and 80 percent said that they had undergone abortions. It is known that 33 percent of all first-born children in the United States between 1964 and 1966 were conceived out of wedlock.

The abortion laws that cause so much suffering obviously apply only to women because they are the ones who have babies. Surprisingly, there are other restrictive laws that apply only to women and have nothing to do with sex at all.

# CHAPTER NINE
# THE LAW AND POLITICS

Sometimes laws discriminate outright against women.

Did you know that in Florida, a married woman who wants to go into business must file a petition in court stating her character, habits, education, mental capacities, and the reasons the judge should grant her request. There is no such requirement for her husband. (There are similar laws in California, Nevada, and Pennsylvania.)

In four states—Arizona, Louisiana, Nevada, and New Mexico—both the husband's and wife's earnings are joint property—and everything is controlled by the husband. In every state, a wife's residence is said to be where her husband lives. If he moves and she chooses not to go with him, she may be guilty of desertion.

In some states, a female prisoner may receive a longer sentence than a male who commits the same crime. In fact, some acts are crimes only if performed by women. In New York, for example, a sixteen-year-old girl can be put in a reform school for up to four years for having sexual experiences with a number of boys (as many as the court decides is "promiscuous"). Such girls are considered "ungovernable and unmanageable"; there is no such penalty for boys.

Numerous states have laws restricting the hours a woman can work or the weights shc can lift. This effectively prevents many women from competing for better-paying jobs or from earning lucrative overtime pay. In ten states, a woman cannot be a bartender, though there are fourteen thousand women bartenders in the rest of the country.

In Alabama, Florida, Indiana, North Carolina, and Texas, a woman cannot sell her own property without her husband's consent. In Georgia, she cannot use her property as collateral for a loan. All these laws, remnants from the time when women had no civil rights at all, exist as handicaps, nuisances, and insults to women. They treat women as incompetent children, punish them harshly for "improper" behavior, and set men over them as protectors and masters.

One of the reasons for such discrimination is that women do not have much say in making the laws. In 1970, women held only 13 seats out of the 535 in Congress. They were less than 5 percent of all state legislators and only .5 percent of the cities' mayors.

A survey conducted by the Office of Women's Activities of the Democratic National Committee (there is no "Office of *Men's* Activities) found that women had a difficult time getting party and financial support to conduct campaigns. One woman, a state senator, said she had to work twice as hard and raise twice as much money. Once elected, she said, "you have to keep fighting to prove yourself as if you didn't have a brain in your head."

Another one-time candidate declared that "most younger married women who are candidates must face the rumor each time that they are pregnant and will not be able to fulfill the rigors of the office which they are seeking." Many candidates who had lost said that they had been chosen as "sacrificial lambs" in districts that had always voted for the other party. One woman reported that her opponent had run an advertisement that said that that particular county was "noted for the good men it has sent to the legislature. . . . Let's keep it that way."

In a speech before the House of Representatives, New York Congresswoman Shirley Chisholm declared, "As a black person, I am no stranger to race prejudice. But the truth is that in the political world I have been far oftener discriminated against because I am a woman than because I am black." And Representative Edith Green of Oregon recalls in disgust that when she was first elected to Congress, newspaper photographers wanted to take her picture in the kitchen. "I asked them to show me pictures of male Congressmen in the kitchen."

Women are also conspicuous by their absence in high policy-making positions in government. Frances Perkins was Secretary of Labor under Franklin Delano Roosevelt, and Oveta Culp Hobby served as Secretary of Health, Education, and Welfare in the administration of Dwight D. Eisenhower. However, there is no woman in the Nixon cabinet.

In 1969, Congresswoman Florence Dwyer of New Jersey sent a letter to President Nixon charging that "This administration has done nothing of significance in the field of women's rights, responsibilities, and opportunities. Not a single important policy decision or legislative recommendation advancing women's rights has been made. Not only have fewer women been appointed to responsible positions than in past Administrations, but the number of existing women office holders replaced by men in the present Administration has reduced the net record to minus one." Congresswoman Dwyer, like the president, is a Republican.

By 1970, President Nixon had appointed only about a dozen women to the ranks of some 850 top office holders—and some of those were in traditional "women's jobs" such as Director of the Women's Bureau, United States Treasurer, and delegate to the United Nations Social Commission of the Economic and Social Council. Only five of the 333 Federal District Court judges in the United States were women. And there was just one woman among the 92 Federal Circuit Court Judges. For some 180 years of existence, there has never been a woman member of the Supreme Court.

*Washington Post* columnist Nicholas von Hoffman scored "the conspicuous example of our President [Nixon] who makes the customary insincere speeches about what he and his party do for women and then continually cuts them out by transacting much of his business at stag or stud affairs, or whatever it is they call those gruesome all-male functions he attends."

There are many reasons—and many myths—to explain why women are not in the seats of policy-making power. Some women do not seek those spots, because they are told it is "unfeminine" to mix in politics or wield executive power. Some voters do not vote for women, because they have bought the myth of feminine inferiority—they think women just are not as capable as men. Women are not appointed to top jobs for the same reasons—and because it is thought they cannot (or should not) supervise men in jobs below them; or because it is thought that women do not have the stamina or drive to compete and hold their own in "a man's world."

As long as people hold these erroneous ideas, women will remain second-class citizens. That is why the feminist debate deals not only with the justice of equal pay for equal work or the need for child-care centers, or the right of every woman to control her own body, but with the deeper philosophical and psychological questions of the nature of woman and her role in this society.

# CHAPTER TEN
# THE WOMAN HATERS

"Woman is by aptitude/destined to servitude . . ."

That is the beginning of a Welsh poem written in the 1500's called "Against Women," and the author was perfectly serious in his view. In fact, the work probably did not arouse much comment—it was written in the wake of a centuries-old tradition of "misogyny"—hatred and contempt for women—that began in ancient times.

In the Greek myth of "Pandora's Box," a woman is made responsible for all the misery and hardship in the world. The Greek philosopher Plato wrote that women were less intelligent than men—he actually wondered whether women could be considered reasonable beings or if they ought to be put in the same category as animals.

Aristotle, another Greek philosopher, thought that woman might have been born because of some mishap during a woman's pregnancy. But no matter what the reason for woman's existence, he was certain about her place: "It is proper for the man to command, for the woman to obey." Originally, pagan religions worshipped women, but at some time, in an era we know little about, the goddesses were replaced by gods and male supremacy in religion was established. It is a characteristic of all major religions, Eastern and Western, and some people believe that the Judaeo-Christian concept of the subservience of women has had great influence on the status of women today.

The Biblical story of Adam and Eve for example, is like the Greek myth of Pandora—woman is responsible for all the sorrow and suffering in the world. It is ironic for misogynists to claim that woman is ignorant when Eve's supposed sin was a desire for knowledge. The other interpretation, of course, is that Eve's sin was sexual. In the Bible, "knowledge" is often used to mean sexual intercourse. The early religious teachers believed that sexual intercourse was sinful and something to engage in only for the purpose of producing children.

The men who wrote the Bible condemned Eve. The Book of Genesis, in the Bible, states: "Unto the woman Eve he said, 'I will multiply greatly thy sorrow and thy conception; in sorrow shall thou bring forth children and thy desire shall be to thy husband, and he shall rule over thee.' "

In the nineteenth century, that passage was cited by the church when it argued against the use of anaesthesia to reduce the pain of childbirth.

Other sections of the Bible declare, "All wickedness is but little to the wickedness of a woman," and "What else is woman but a foe to friendship, an unescapable punishment, a necessary evil, a natural temptation, a desirable calamity, a domestic danger, a delectable detriment, an evil of nature, painted with fair colours!"

Christ, incidentally, said virtually nothing at all about woman and her place, and he showed more compassion for the suffering of the prostitute (Mary Magdalene) than did his followers in centuries to come.

Much of early Christian misogyny derived from the Jewish variety. Jewish women lived subject to their husbands and fathers; in fact, an Orthodox Jewish prayer today reflects the attitude men held toward women then. It declares, "Blessed art thou O Lord our God, King of the Universe who has not made me a woman."

One explanation for this contempt for women is that the early churchmen—like the men in primitive cultures—were afraid of women's sexuality. They were afraid of their own desire for women and therefore accused women of "tempting" them. Some went so far as to say that it was all a plot of the devil.

For example, the Muslim teacher Muhammad said, "When Eve was created, Satan rejoiced." The Persian prophet Zoroaster said that sex made women diabolical. Saint Jerome declared, "Woman is the true Satan, the foe of peace, the subject of dissension." The Jewish King Solomon asserted, "Who can find a virtuous woman, for her price is far above rubies." And the Hindu Code of Manu declared: "In childhood a woman must be subject to her father; in youth to her husband; when her husband is dead, to her sons. A woman must never be free of subjugation."

Saint Paul, considered one of the prime woman-haters of his day, said that man was not created for women, but that woman was created for man. He also had a loathing of sex and said, "It is not good for a man to touch a woman." However, he recommended that people get married if they could not overcome their sexual instincts. ("It is better to marry than to burn.")

He also disliked women who spoke for themselves—especially when they disagreed with men. "Let the women learn in silence with all subjection," he declared. "Wives, submit yourselves to your husbands."

Saint Paul's letter of instructions to the Corinthians established the place of woman—on the bottom. "The head of every man is Christ; and the head of the woman is the man," he told them.

Saint Augustine, another early misogynist, described woman as a temple built over a sewer. He also believed that virginity was better than marriage. Saint Jerome modified this somewhat: marriage might be approved, but only because it brought new virgins into the world.

If marriage existed, he believed, it should be to produce children, certainly not for pleasure. He counseled widows who wanted to remarry to "confess your vileness. No woman marries with the idea of not sleeping with a husband," he declared, adding, "If you (already) have children, why do you want to marry?"

Later, in eleventh-century Italy, there were actually debates over whether women had souls.

During the early days of Christianity, women were allowed to preach, baptize, and perform other religious functions. By the Middle Ages, everything had changed, and the Christian Church resembled the male-dominated Jewish religion where women were so little regarded that prayers could be conducted only when at least ten men were present (women did not count). Even in some synagogues today, women who attend services must sit in a back section or on a balcony behind drawn curtains.

There were, however, some churchmen who did not agree with their colleagues. Sir Thomas More, who lived in the early 1500's, believed that women and men were equal and that women should be allowed to become priests.

During the Renaissance a writer named Torquato Tasso put the male supremacist viewpoint very succinctly: "Every woman would wish to be a man, just as every deformed wretch would wish to be whole and fair and as every idiot and fool would wish to be learned and wise." And the poet John Milton wondered why God had even put this "defect of nature" on earth instead of populating the world only with men and finding "some other way to generate mankind."

Misogyny became a primary occupation for some men. In the 1480's, Jacob Sprenger and Heinrich Kramer wrote a book called *Malleus Maleficarum* (Witches' Hammer) which used religious doctrine as the basis for a brutal attack on women that some say caused the beginning of the witchcraft mania.

According to their book, "There was a defect in the formation of the first woman since she was formed from a bent rib. Through this defect she is an imperfect animal," and "she always deceives."

Besides being called liars, women were said to have inferior intelligence and to be filled with sexual lust—two of the main themes of misogyny. In fact, *Malleus Maleficarum*—a very influential book in its time—said that witches were women who had intercourse with the devil and that they could make men impotent, unable to have sexual intercourse, by damaging their sexual organs.

If anyone wondered why only women became witches, the answer was that "they are feebler both in mind and body" than men, and "all witchcraft comes from carnal lust which is in women insatiable." The witchcraft mania was a logical conclusion of some men's hatred and contempt for women and their fear of sex. Unfortunately, the aberration resulted in more than some nasty books. In seventeenth-century England, a Witchfinder General was appointed to supervise witch-hunters who were paid to round up victims. Anyone who dared be different or assert her independence was liable to be denounced as a witch and hanged or burned alive.

The Protestant Reformation in the sixteenth century did nothing to change the official church attitudes about women. Martin Luther believed that it was natural for women to be secondary to men. He also thought that sexual relations carried on Original Sin. John Calvin, too, was contemptuous of women; the only useful function he thought they had was bearing children—as many as possible. In fact, he favored polygamy so that fewer women would remain unwed and childless.

Calvin spoke against political equality for women, declaiming that the rule of women would be a "deviation from the original and proper order of nature." He made an exception of Queen Elizabeth, whom he said had been "raised by Divine Authority."

John Knox, a sixteenth-century Scottish statesman, was not so careful. When he wrote "The First Blast of the Trumpet Against the Monstrous Regiment of Women," he did not take into account the reaction of female monarchs. Reigning Queen Mary died shortly after the piece was published, but Elizabeth I, of England barred Knox from that country. John Aylmer, the Bishop of London, answered Knox's attack by pointing out that the queens of England had been greater than any of the sovereigns that had ever ruled the nation before.

In "Man Superior to Woman or a Vindication of Man's Natural Right of Sovereign Authority Over the Woman," an anonymous author, in 1739, ran through the familiar litany of female faults. "So dangerous is a little understanding to that tender Sex! How happy is it for them that Learning but seldom molests them. What strange Distraction would it not create in their poor tender Heads. . . . They, alas, poor pretty Creatures, have neither Breath nor Brains to drink of Knowledge deeply."

"Women's conversation is inspired by 'venom,' " said the author, asserting that it is made up of "scandal, indecency, hypocrisy, or impiety." Women act out of "perversity," he said, and seldom fail to "jilt" men. Perhaps that last blast gives a clue to the source of the gentleman's dissatisfaction.

The eighteenth-century French philosopher Jean Jacques Rousseau had some almost sadistic notions about the extent of woman's required subservience. He began with the assumption that women ought to be obedient to men and he discussed the methods of instilling such discipline. It was, he said, "necessary to accustom them early to such confinement, that it may not afterwards cost them too dear; and to the suppression of their caprices that they may the more readily submit to the will of others."

He declared, "She ought to learn even to suffer injustices and to bear the insults of a husband without complaint." He added charitably, "It is not necessary to make her dependence burdensome, but only to let her feel it."

Through the centuries, there was a good deal written about the necessity of *whipping* women. The Russians believed that periodic beating was good for a woman's character, and the domestic law of the 1500's allowed men to beat their wives if they were not absolutely obedient. Later, the nineteenth-century German philosopher, Friedrich Nietzsche, advised, "When you go to a woman, do not forget to take along your whip." Whether or not men talked about it, wife-beating was common and legal in all parts of the world and was not a valid reason for a woman to obtain a divorce.

The Enlightenment of the eighteenth century did not have a great effect on men's attitudes toward women. French philosopher Diderot declared: "Women prefer lustful, depraved men because women are depraved and lustful." And English statesman Edmund Burke noted, "A woman is but an animal and not an animal of the highest order." Even the great liberal Thomas Jefferson said in 1807, "The appointment of a woman to office is an innovation for which the public is not prepared—nor am I."

Into the late 1800's, prominent male thinkers seriously argued the inferiority of the female sex. The philosophers Nietzsche and Schopenhauer, the playwright August Strindberg, and the psychoanalyst Sigmund Freud are sterling examples of that school of thought.

Nietzsche believed that there was an eternal war between men and women that prevented the possibility of equality. Peace in that conflict would only come when one party was established as the master. Women, he said, would be content with subordination, especially if they achieved their ultimate destiny—motherhood. "Everything in woman is a riddle," he said, "and everything in woman hath one answer; its name is childbearing."

Schopenhauer called women "childish, frivolous and short-sighted

—in a word, they are big children all their life long," he said, "preferring trifles to matters of the first importance." He charged them with "falsity, faithlessness, treachery, and ingratitude," said they had no talent or appreciation for the arts and should be brought up to be submissive housewives. "Women exist in the main solely for the propagation of the species and are not destined for anything else," he added emphatically.

Because "women are defective in the powers of reasoning and deliberation," Schopenhauer declared, they have "no sense of justice" and he suggested that they should not be allowed to testify in court. He noted curiously that women's small reasoning capacity "explains why it is that women show more sympathy for the unfortunate than men do and so treat them with more kindness and interest." As if compassion was weakness.

August Strindberg, who had three unhappy marriages, announced that women were not oppressed. He explained, "Nature has ordained that she should live under the protection of the man while she fulfills her mission in life as mother."

"Woman is not man's intellectual equal; the man, on the other hand, cannot bear children," he argued. "She is not an essential factor in the great work of civilization; this is man's domain, for he is better fitted to grapple with spiritual problems than she is." Strindberg did not think any woman should work as long as it was man's role to provide for his wife and family—and he appeared to think that role was eternal.

Strindberg further asserted that women did not deserve to be equal with men since they had not created the ideals, art, professions, and culture of civilization. (He said nothing about the poverty and warfare men had managed to create along the way.)

Sigmund Freud may easily be the most dangerous and destructive misogynist of this generation. He died in 1939, but his influence lives on in his books, his disciples, and countless articles, and through popular catchphrases that are part of peoples' everyday lives and conversations. Freud's theory of women's inferiority centers around the concept of "penis envy." Freud believed that women were jealous of men because they did not have penises. When a woman said she was unhappy staying at home and doing housework, or frustrated because she could not get a good job, Freud blamed it all on penis envy. Any woman who wanted a career and independence, he explained, was really trying to be a man. (Ironically, his daughter Anna became a famous psychiatrist.)

The only true role for women is motherhood, declared Freud. And what a woman really needs is a son to whom she can transfer all the ambition she has had to suppress in herself. He made his ideas clear in letters he wrote to his fiancée. "It seems a completely unrealistic notion to send women into the struggle for existence in the same way as men," he declared. "Am I to think of my delicate sweet girl as a competitor?"

Freud criticized his fiancée's mother for wanting to live her own life. He said, "As a mother, she ought to be content to know that her three children are fairly happy, and she ought to sacrifice her wishes to their needs." "And," he added, "the portion of woman cannot be other than what it is: to be an adored sweetheart in youth and a beloved wife in maturity." He made no mention of the untold numbers of women who did not marry, who were widows, or who were tyrannized, beaten, or deserted by their husbands.

Like Strindberg and others, Freud believed that women lacked "a sense of justice"—again, a result of penis envy. In fact, for Sigmund Freud, penis envy was rather like the old patent medicine that general stores used to dispense on the frontier—it was a good answer for just about everything.

Modern misogyny reached its heights in Nazi Germany, which was famous for its dictum that woman's place was with children, in the kitchen, and in church ("Kinder, Küche, Kirche"). In fact, Hitler declared that the idea of women's emancipation was a Jewish plot.

"Her world is her husband, her family, her children, and her home," Hitler declared. "We do not find it right when the woman presses into the world of the man. Rather, we find it natural when these two worlds remain separate. . . . To one belongs the power of feeling, the power of the soul (misogynists never could agree on whether women had no soul or more soul). . . . To the other belongs the strength of vision, the strength of hardness. . . . The equal rights of women consist in the fact that in the realm of life determined for her by nature, she experiences the highest esteem that is her due."

Hitler continued the old myth of women's intellectual inferiority. "Woman and man represent two quite different types of being," he said. "Reason is dominant in man. He searches, analyzes, and often opens new immeasurable realms."

Nazi propaganda minister Joseph Paul Goebbels echoed similar thoughts. "The National Socialist movement is in its nature a masculine movement," he declared. Politics, he said, was a man's world. "When we eliminate women from public life, it is not because we want to dispense with them, but because we want to give them back their essential honor. . . . The outstanding and highest calling of woman is always that of wife and mother, and it would be unthinkable misfortune if we allowed ourselves to be turned from this point of view."

To make sure that women stayed at home, the Nazis limited women's suffrage, excluded women from public office, set a quota on women in universities, purged them from the Reichstag (there had been thirty women delegates), and made contraception and abortion illegal. (In Russia, Stalin also banned abortions.)

One of the most prominent present-day sexists is baby doctor Benjamin Spock who would like to convince women that their most important role is taking care of children. "If we don't, and more and more women go to college, who the hell is going to take care of the children?" he says worriedly.

If women do work, he thinks they ought to take helpful jobs like those of secretaries and nurses. He says women are more patient in working at unexciting, repetitive tasks. "Man is the fighter, the builder, the trap-maker, the one who thinks mechanically and abstractly." Men are the natural leaders, he says, ". . . men stay more analytic and cool."

In our time, democratic philosophies have developed new ideas about every person's right to fulfill their potential and to seek happiness and satisfaction according to their own interests and talents. However, several thousand years of misogyny cannot be erased so quickly. People still repeat the old myths about woman's inferiority. They still insist that it is man's place to rule the world and woman's to sweep the floor and cook dinner. Yet, there have always been women and men who have fought for women's equality. Their story is part of the proud history of womankind.

*"I ask no favors for my sex. I surrender not our claim to equality. All I ask of our brethren is that they will take their feet from off our necks and permit us to stand upright on the ground which God has designed us to occupy!"*

*Angelina Grimke (1805–1879)*

# CHAPTER ELEVEN WOMEN IN EARLY HISTORY

In 215 B.C., Roman women organized and lobbied against the Lex Oppia which limited the amount of gold they could own and forbade them to ride in carriages within a mile of Rome except on festival days. They canvassed voters and demonstrated at the homes of their opponents. And they won their demands.

The oppression of women has existed in more than the misogynist rantings of orators and authors. It has been entrenched in law, in economic practice, and in social customs, and through the years of their subjugation, women have fought back with words and deeds in the struggle for their equality.

It is not necessarily a story of continual improvement. In some past ages, women lost power they had once possessed or were robbed of rights they had previously enjoyed. For example, archaeologists digging in the ruins at Pompeii discovered slogans on the walls calling for the election of women who were candidates for city office. Centuries later, there and elsewhere, women could not even vote.

In prehistorical times, it is believed that men and women may have lived communally, without pairing off as husband and wife. The men, who were stronger, did the hunting, and the women, who were subject to continual pregnancy, nursed their children and cooked food for the family. Later, when the development of agriculture forced people to give up their nomadic way of life and settle down, men staked out land for themselves—and they also staked out their own wives. Woman may have been one of the earliest examples of private property.

Women continued to be literally the property of men for centuries. Thousands of years ago, Hebrew women lived under the rule of their fathers who sold them to the men who became their husbands. Marriage was a business deal and adultery was really a kind of trespassing —it violated someone's private property.

Things were not very different among other peoples at that time. In ancient Babylon, once a year young women were auctioned off to the highest bidders, who then became their husbands. The prettiest were sold first, so that the men would have an opportunity to pick up the leftovers if they were outbid on their first choices. The wedding ring remains as a symbol of the old "bride price."

The Greek city-states practiced a variety of attitudes toward women. In Sparta, women and men could inherit property equally, and women owned 40 percent of the land. Some women had two husbands and lived alternately in two households. In Athens, however, women were confined to their homes. They could not go out in the streets or appear in public, and their husbands preferred the company of "*hetaerae*," personable, educated, women who were often from other cities and acted as courtesans to entertain the men, who were bored by their own cloistered wives.

Roman women were barred from public office, though they had rights to their property. Women were part of the *familia*, the household belonging to one man, his wife, children, and servants or slaves; and he had the power of life and death over all of them. The word "family," in fact, comes from the Latin *famulus*, which means servant.

During the Punic Wars, many of the men were away and the women, who had greater responsibility for running their households, used the occasion to win greater rights for themselves. They were allowed to inherit property, though in 169 B.C. a law was passed limiting the amount of wealth women could inherit. Women took part in activities outside the home, became active in politics and religious movements, studied philosophy, and even attended military maneuvers. Conservatives and "male chauvinists" echoed the age-old cry that they were following "male pursuits." Most of this emancipation affected only the women of the upper classes, but it was an early sign that women were not satisfied with the role that men had assigned them.

Hebrew culture was an unremitting patriarchy, with husbands having total power over their wives and children. Christianity borrowed much from the Hebrews in theology—and it continued the theory and practice of women's subjugation.

In early Christian times women lost what few rights they had won from the Romans. One churchman even sought to limit the kinds of physical exercise women could have, denying them the sports and athletics men enjoyed. In "The Instructor," Saint Clement declared that women "are not to be encouraged to engage in wrestling or running, but are to exercise themselves in spinning, weaving, and superintending the cooking." Other advice for healthful exercise was fetching food from the storehouse, milling, and making the home comfortable for one's husband.

In A.D. 439, Theodosius II issued a law allowing husbands to divorce wives for disobeying them and for visiting the theater, the circus, or other public places. In sixth- through eleventh-century England men were in command, but women were allowed to inherit property. Women also began to be allowed to refuse to marry men that had been chosen as their husbands if they were insane, had leprosy, were criminals, or were objectionable for other serious reasons. However, their fathers had the last word on whether the objections were valid.

During the next five hundred years in medieval England, women lost some of their property rights. Everything came under the control of their husbands with a pronouncement that said, "It is adjudged that the wife has nothing of her own while her husband lives." The law codified what society already practiced. In 1365, the jurists of the Middle Ages decreed that women could have no personal identity, and English common law, as later written down by Blackstone, provided that: "By marriage, the husband and wife are one person in the law—that is, the very being or legal existence of the woman is suspended during the marriage." Husband and wife were one, all right—and that one was the husband.

As a result, any lawsuits against the wife had to be filed against her husband. Neither could she sue. Since a husband was liable for damages caused by his wife's "misbehavior," he had the right to take the necessary steps to keep her in line. Church law allowed husbands to beat wives with whips and cudgels, though there was a prohibition against knocking women down with iron bars.

When Joan of Arc led the French army into battle in 1429, she proved that even the oppression and degradation of centuries could not stifle the brilliance of leadership of at least the most extraordinary women. Yet, even she was brought down by the authorities and burned at the stake for her impudence. Imagine to what heights of national and international prominence she might have risen if only she had been born a man.

When Queen Elizabeth came to the English throne, she brought with her a period of greater freedom for women—at least compared to their sisters on the continent. "The females have great liberty and are almost like their masters," declared a visitor, Frederick, Duke of Wurtemberg, in 1592. However, the next century was the era of the witch hysteria, an antiwoman terror that spread from Europe to the United States, where the Salem witch trials symbolized the awful penalties paid by women who dared to be different.

Throughout those years, there were women and men who spoke up against the subjugation of women. A Dutch woman, Anna Maria à Schurman, wrote a book in 1659 challenging the notion that women ought to be servants to men. An English woman named Mary Astell, in 1696 published "An Essay in Defense of the Female Sex," which talked about the loss of freedom by women in marriage.

In sixteenth-, seventeenth-, and eighteenth-century England, there were the beginnings of feminist protest, but women were still legally subject to men. In 1681, Lord Halifax summed up the general male supremacist opinion when he instructed women in their role. "You must first lay it down for a foundation in general that there is inequality in the sexes and that for the better economy of the world, the men, who were to be the law-givers, had the larger share of reason bestowed upon them, by which means your sex is the better prepared for the compliance that is necessary for the better performance of those duties which seem to be most properly assigned to it."

He admitted that, ". . . this looks a little uncourtly at the first appearance, but upon examination it will be found that Nature is so far from being unjust to you that she is partial on your side. She hath made you such large amends by other advantages, for the seeming injustice of the first distribution, that the right of complaining is come over to our sex; you have it in your power not only to free yourselves, but to subdue your masters, and without violence throw both their natural and legal authority at your feet."

Thus, he told women who had no legal rights or the opportunity to earn their livings as anything but maids or governesses that even though they were mentally deficient, they really had the best of things because they could easily have men swooning at their feet. His comments were not likely to be much comfort to a poverty-stricken widow with five children, or to a wife who was cheated out of her inheritance or her own earnings by an unscrupulous husband.

A century later, another "helpful" Englishman informed women that "to make a good husband is but one branch of a man's duty; but it is the chief duty of a woman to make a good wife." He suggested that "woman, destined to be obedient, ought to be disciplined early to bear wrongs without murmuring. This is a hard lesson, and yet it is necessary for their own sake."

One of the pioneer thinkers of women's liberation was Mary Wollstonecraft of England, who in 1792, in a famous book called *A Vindication of the Rights of Women,* challenged every kind of slander that had been directed against her sex. It was reprinted repeatedly in the following centuries and is available even today.

"Women are rendered weak and wretched," she said, as their "strength and usefulness are sacrificed to beauty. . . . They are treated as a kind of subordinate being. . . . Men endeavor to sink us still lower," she charged, "merely to render us alluring objects. . . . Man taking her body, the mind is left to rust.

"Men, in their youth, are prepared for professions, and marriage is not considered as the grand feature in their lives, while women, on the contrary, have no other scheme to sharpen their faculties," she declared. "To rise in the world and have the liberty of running from pleasure to pleasure, they must marry advantageously, and to this object their time is sacrificed and their persons often legally prostituted.

"Should they be beautiful, everything else is needless for at least twenty years of their lives," for women believe it is only through their ability "to excite emotions in men that pleasure and power are to be obtained." She asked, "Why are women to be thus bred up with a desire for conquest? The very word used in this sense gives me a sickly qualm!" She said she did not wish women to have power over men, but over themselves.

"How many women thus waste life away the prey of discontent, who might have practiced as physicians, regulated a farm, managed a shop, and stood erect, supported by their own industry.

"The few employments open to women, far from being liberal, are menial; and when a superior education enables them to take charge of the education of children as governesses, they are not treated like the tutors of sons."

She insisted that a woman "must not be dependent on her husband's bounty for her subsistence during his life or support after his death." If women had their own incomes, it "might save many from common and legal prostitution. Women would not then marry for support," she said. They would not be forced "to escape in this pitiful way from servitude."

As for the notion that such pursuits were "masculine," she responded that "the word masculine is only a bugbear." And if it is masculine to attain those virtues that raise women above the level of animals, she said she wished that women "may every day grow more and more masculine."

And, she noted that the description of the "perfect woman" drawn by a contemporary misogynist was ". . . the portrait of a house slave . . . Such a woman," she said, "ought to be an angel—or she is an ass—for I discern not a trace of the human character, neither reason nor passion, in this domestic drudge whose being is absorbed in that of a tyrant's."

On the other side of the Atlantic Ocean, the women of the colonies and then of the new United States faced similar obstacles to equality, as the roles of the sexes were interpreted to make women the inferiors and servants of men.

One year before Mary Wollstonecraft's book came out, Judith Sargent Stevens Murray, of Gloucester, Massachusetts, using the pseudonym of Constantia, had written: "Will it be said that the judgment of a male of two years old is more sage than that of a female of the same age? I believe the reverse is generally observed to be true. But from that period what partiality! How is the one exalted and the other depressed by the contrary modes of education which are adopted! The one is taught to aspire and the other is early confined and limited.

"I would calmly ask, is it reasonable that a candidate for immortality, for the joys of heaven, an intelligent being who is to spend an eternity in contemplating the works of Deity, should at present be so degraded as to be allowed no other ideas than those which are suggested by the mechanism of a pudding or the sewing of the seams of a garment?" she declared, and deplored the customs by which women are "adorned with ribbons and other gewgaws, dressed out like the ancient victims previous to a sacrifice, being taught by the care of our parents in collecting the most showy materials that the ornamentation of our exterior ought to be the principle object of our attention."

In 1799, English readers could buy "The Female Advocate, or an Attempt to Recover the Right of Women from Male Usurpation," by Mary Anna Radcliffe, who expressed her concern at the fact that women were not educated or trained so that they could earn their own livings.

There were some who did earn their own livings, of course, but they never got the recognition or credit of men who did similar work. You have heard of Benjamin Franklin, but what about his sister Ann, who was the first woman newspaper editor in America and ran the *Newport Mercury* in Rhode Island? Or Catherine Green, who has been called the true inventor of "Eli Whitney's" cotton gin? While history says that Whitney was a guest of Mrs. Green's when he developed the cotton gin, there are some people who believe that Mrs. Green patented the invention in Whitney's name out of fear that society would ridicule her for showing "masculine" talents.

(In later years, thousands of patents were awarded to women inventors; many other discoveries were registered in the names of women's husbands and their employees.)

The eighteenth century was the time of the Enlightenment in Europe, of the French and American revolutions, of slogans that promised "liberty and justice for all." However, women learned fast enough that the slogans were not meant to apply to them. In America, Abigail Adams wrote to her husband John, "In the new code of laws which I suppose it will be necessary for you to make, I desire you would remember the ladies and be more generous and favorable to them than your ancestors. Do not put such unlimited power into the hands of the husband. Remember, all men would be tyrants if they could." And she warned, "If particular care and attention is not paid to the ladies, we are determined to foment a rebellion and will not hold ourselves bound by any laws in which we have no voice or representation."

The man who became the second president of the United States responded with the tired old line about women really running the world because they run their husbands: "In practice, you know we have only the name of masters and rather than give this up, which would completely subject us to the despotism of the petticoat, I hope General Washington and all our brave heroes would fight."

However, the American revolutionaries were not all so insensitive. Thomas Paine described the sorrowful condition of women, ". . . . even in countries where they may be esteemed the most happy, constrained in their desires, in the disposal of their goods, robbed of freedom and will by the laws . . . surrounded on all sides by judges who are at once tyrants and their seducers."

It was in the mid-1800's that the demands for women's rights that had been raised sporadically since the times of ancient Greece and Rome seemed to win increasing numbers of adherents, and feminism stopped being just an intellectual argument; it started being a movement.

The demands of the movement were similar in each country. Women wanted control over their own property and earnings, equal rights to their own children, divorce reform, opportunities in employment and education, and the legal status to sue and testify in court.

In the United States, the feminist movement gained impetus from the organizations formed to press for the abolition of slavery. (Black abolitionist leader Frederick Douglass was a staunch feminist.) Many women got their political and "soap box" training from the antislavery movement, but ironically, the first major women's rights convention was called as a result of their exclusion from participation in antislavery societies on an equal basis with men.

When the American Anti-Slavery Society was founded in Philadelphia in 1833, women attended the meeting—but they were barred from membership. Lucretia Mott and others promptly organized their own Philadelphia Female Anti-Slavery Society.

When Sarah and Angelina Grimke toured New England to speak against slavery in 1836, the Council of Congregational Ministers of Massachusetts issued a statement attacking them and pointing out that "The power of a woman is her dependency flowing from the consciousness of that weakness which God has given her for her protection." It declared that "when she assumes the place and tone of man as a public reformer, she yields the power which God has given her for her protection and her character becomes unnatural."

The answer came swift and sharp from Sarah Grimke, who retorted: " 'Her influence is the source of mighty power!' This has ever been the flattering language of man since he laid aside the whip as a means to keep woman in subjection. He spares her body; but the war he has waged against her mind, her heart and her soul has been no less destructive to her as a moral being. How monstrous is the doctrine that woman is to be dependent on man!

"It will scarcely be denied," she said, "that as a general rule men do not desire the improvement of women. There are few instances of men who are magnanimous enough to be entirely willing that women should know more than themselves on any subjects except dress and cookery. As *they* have determined that Jehovah has placed woman on a lower platform than man, they of course wish to keep her there; and hence the noble faculties of our minds are crushed and our reasoning powers are almost wholly uncultivated." She said their attitude could "justly be placed on a par with the policy of the slaveholder who says that men will be better slaves if they are not permitted to learn to read."

# CHAPTER TWELVE THE RIGHT TO EDUCATION

Jean Jacques Rousseau thought very little of women's intellectual abilities. "Almost all of them learn with reluctance to read and write; but very readily apply themselves to the use of their needles." With such feeble brains, they were obviously unfit for "researches into abstract and speculative truths, the principles and axioms of sciences, in short, everything which tends to generalize our ideas."

He said, "The whole education of women ought to be relative to men. To please them, to be useful to them, to make themselves loved and honored by them, to educate them when young, to care for them when grown, to counsel them, to console them, and to make life sweet and agreeable to them—these are the duties of women at all times and what should be taught them from their infancy."

It sounds outrageous now, but that was an opinion held by most people of that time. It was generally believed, in fact, that women's brains were smaller than men's and therefore inferior.

Since early history, men seem to have been afraid of intelligent women. The Greek playwright Euripides wrote: "A clever woman I hate! May there never be in my house a woman more intellectual than a woman ought to be." In Elizabethan England, writers argued that beauty was given to women to compensate for their feeble intelligence.

If women were taught anything—and such education was limited to the wealthy—it was in such arts as painting, embroidery, singing, speaking French, and playing musical instruments. Subjects like science and mathematics were considered too taxing for their limited brains!

Yet even hundreds of years ago, women fought and protested against those myths. Here is a poem written by Lady Winchilsea, an English noblewoman born in 1661:

*How are we fallen! Fallen by mistaken rules*
*And Education's more than Nature's fools;*
*Debarred from all improvements of the mind,*
*And to be dull, expected and designed;*
*And if some one would soar above the rest,*
*With warmer fancy and ambitions pressed,*
*So strong the opposing faction still appears,*
*The hopes to thrive can ne'er outweigh the fears.*

*Alas! A woman that attempts the pen,*
*Such a presumptuous creature is esteemed,*
*The fault can by no virtue be redeemed.*
*They tell us we mistake our sex and way;*
*Good breeding, fashion, dancing, dressing, play,*
*Are the accomplishments we should desire;*
*To write or read or think or to enquire,*
*Would cloud our beauty, and exhaust our time,*
*And interrupt the conquests of our prime,*
*Whilst the dull manage of a servile house*
*Is held by some our utmost art and use.*

And on the other side of the Atlantic in 1642, Anne Bradstreet had written:

*I am obnoxious to each carping tongue*
*Who sayes, my hand a needle better fits,*
*A Poets Pen, all scorne, I should thus wrong;*
*For such despight they cast on female wits:*
*If what I doe prove well, it won't advance,*
*They'll say it's stolne, or else, it was by chance.*

English novelist Virginia Woolf wrote in *A Room of One's Own* that when ". . . one reads of a witch being dunked, of a woman possessed by devils . . . then I think we are on the track of a lost novelist and a suppressed poet, of some mute and inglorious Jane Austen. . . . Indeed, I would venture to guess that 'Anon.,' who wrote so many poems without signing them, was often a woman."

Public opinion on the subject of female intelligence was not much improved by the 1700's. Here is some advice from Dr. Gregory's "Legacy to His Daughters":

"Be even cautious in displaying your good sense. It will be thought you assume a superiority over the rest of the company. But if you happen to have any learning, keep it a profound secret, especially from the men, who generally look with a jealous and malignant eye on a woman of great parts and a cultivated understanding."

Let anyone dare ask why there have not been, in the course of history, as many great women writers and thinkers as men! Learning was considered unfeminine! Novelist Jane Austen's nephew wrote in 1800 that "She was careful that her occupation should not be suspected by servants or visitors or any persons beyond her own family party." Many of the visitors to that house never knew that she was the brilliant creator of *Pride and Prejudice*.

And why do you think Mary Ann Evans, who wrote *The Mill on the Floss* and *Middlemarch* used the pseudonym of a man, George Eliot? Why did Amandine Dupin Dudevairt take the name George Sand?

In Charlotte Brontë's book, *Jane Eyre,* published in 1847, the heroine declares that women need the same opportunity as men to use their brains. "It is narrow-minded in their more privileged fellow-creatures to say that they ought to confine themselves to making puddings and knitting stockings, to playing on the piano, and embroidering bags. It is thoughtless to condemn them, or laugh at them, if they seek to do more or learn more than custom has pronounced necessary for their sex." She first published her books under the name of Currer Bell.

Neither Jane Austen nor George Eliot, nor George Sand, nor Emily nor Charlotte Brontë had children. How many other great "authors" never published books because they were too busy diapering babies?

"Men went into business and made money and left their money to found colleges for their own sex," declared Virginia Woolf. "Even if it had been possible for women to earn money, the law denied them the right to possess that money they earned." She was talking about England, but she could just as well have been describing the conditions in the United States.

The women who fought for the right to vote were also strongly committed to the struggle for equal educational opportunity for women. "What an absurd notion that women have not intellectual and moral faculties sufficient for anything but domestic concerns," asserted Susan B. Anthony when she was twenty years old. She was teaching at a girls' academy—and was paid only a fourth of the salary of the man she had replaced.

When suffragist Elizabeth Cady Stanton was a young girl, she helped raise money to send a youth to a religious seminary. After graduation, he outraged his female benefactor by giving a speech in which he quoted Saint Timothy: "But I suffer not a woman to teach, nor to usurp authority over the man, but to be in silence." She led the others in a walkout and never again raised money for seminary students.

In 1851 a book was published that declared: "A lady should appear to *think* well of books rather than to *speak* well of them." But also in the 1850's, feminists were passing resolutions at women's rights conventions demanding admission to all-male schools and colleges. At that time, women were not even admitted to public high schools! (The conventions called for admission of women to Harvard and Yale—a victory that was only won recently at Yale and not yet at Harvard.)

Black girls had the least opportunity to learn, in the "abolitionist" states as well as in the South. In the 1830's, when Prudence Crandall accepted a black girl into her school in Canterbury, Connecticut, the reaction was violent. She refused to agree to the public's demand to send the girl away, and instead closed down the school. Two months later she reopened it—this time with seventeen black girls as students. After a year of harassment, the school was shut. Today, a women's dormitory at Howard University is named Crandall Hall.

One of the first girls' schools in this country was the Troy Female Seminary organized in 1821 by Emma Willard who thought that girls as well as boys ought to learn algebra, geometry, trigonometry, and the sciences. She had to teach those subjects to herself in order to teach them to others, for she was barred from attending the men's schools that had them in the curriculum.

The first coeducational college in the country was Oberlin, which was founded in 1832 in Ohio. However, even there the first women students took a special literary course—the administrators of Oberlin thought their minds could not handle the same work as men. Suffragist Lucy Stone attended Oberlin, but she refused to write a commencement essay, because it would have had to have been read by a male student.

She wrote: "Oberlin's attitude was that women's high calling was to be the mothers of the race, and that they should stay within that special sphere in order that future generations should not suffer from the want of devoted and undistracted mother care. If women became lawyers, ministers, physicians, lecturers, politicians or any sort of 'public character,' the home would suffer from neglect. . . .

"Washing the men's clothes, caring for their rooms, serving them at table, listening to their orations, but themselves remaining respectfully silent in public assemblages, the Oberlin 'co-eds' were being prepared for intelligent motherhood and a properly subservient wifehood."

Mount Holyoke was founded in 1837 by Mary Lyon who, in order to raise money, had to travel through New England visiting wealthy people and picking up small amounts of money at church meetings and family gatherings. Mount Holyoke rejected that idea that the purpose of women's education was to enable them to be better wives and mothers or to teach. The girls learned English, geography, history, philosophy, chemistry, geology, and the like. That same year, Susan B. Anthony, who was only a seventeen-year-old schoolteacher, was calling for equal pay for women teachers, coeducation, and higher education for women.

In the latter part of the century Vassar, Smith, Wellesley, Bryn Mawr, and other colleges were established because women could not get an education elsewhere. Even in the late 1800's, education for women was a controversial question. M. Carey Thomas, class of Cornell, 1877, and President of Bryn Mawr from 1894 to 1922, recalled that when she went to study at Leipzig after graduation from Cornell, "my mother used to write me that my name was never mentioned to her by the women of her acquaintance. I was thought by them to be as much of a disgrace to my family as if I had eloped with the coachman."

As late as 1913, one generous man noted that "women of genius and talent are not *necessarily* depraved."

And several centuries after Lady Winchilsea's protest, this poem (*Sonnet XXXI*) could be written by Edna St. Vincent Millay (1892–1950):

*Oh, oh, you will be sorry for that word!*
*Give back my book and take my kiss instead.*
*Was it my enemy or my friend I heard,*
*"What a big book for such a little head!"*
*Come, I will show you now my newest hat,*
*And you may watch me purse my mouth and prink!*
*Oh, I shall love you still, and all of that.*
*I never again shall tell you what I think.*
*I shall be sweet and crafty, soft and sly;*
*You will not catch me reading any more:*
*I shall be called a wife to pattern by;*
*And some day when you knock and push the door,*
*Some sane day, not too bright and not too stormy,*
*I shall be gone, and you may whistle for me.*

# CHAPTER THIRTEEN BEGINNINGS OF THE MOVEMENT

In 1840, Lucretia Mott, Elizabeth Cady Stanton and a delegation of American women were barred from participation in a world anti-slavery conference held in London.

The men, who had gathered in the name of freeing black people, argued the question of their participation all day and finally ordered the women to watch the proceedings from a curtained gallery in the back. William Lloyd Garrison refused to take part in the convention and joined the women in protest. And Lucretia Mott and Elizabeth Cady Stanton vowed to return to the United States and do something about the status of their sex.

They both had the traditional family responsibilities, and it was eight years before they organized the first convention on women's rights in Seneca Falls, New York. Mrs. Stanton told the several hundred women and men who gathered there that it was time to put the question of the subjection of women before the public and that "woman herself must do this work, for woman alone can understand the height, the depth, the length and breadth of her degradation."

The Seneca Falls declaration was a stirring statement of the deepest feelings of women and a list of the grievances that women suffered in every area of life. It was modeled after the Declaration of Independence and said in part:

"The history of mankind is a history of repeated injuries and usurpations on the part of man toward woman, having in direct object the establishment of an absolute tyranny over her. To prove this, let facts be submitted to a candid world.

"He has never permitted her to exercise her inalienable right to the elective franchise.

"He has compelled her to submit to laws in the formation of which she had no voice.

"He has withheld from her rights which are given to the most ignorant and degraded men—both natives and foreigners.

"Having deprived her of this first right of a citizen, the elective franchise, thereby leaving her without representation in the halls of legislation, he has oppressed her on all sides.

"He has made her, if married, in the eye of the law, civilly dead.

"He has taken from her all right in property, even to the wages she earns.

"He has made her, morally, an irresponsible being, as she can commit many crimes with impunity, provided they be done in the presence of her husband. In the covenant of marriage, she is compelled to promise obedience to her husband, he becoming, to all intents and purposes, her master—the law giving him power to deprive her of her liberty and to administer chastisement.

"He has so framed the laws of divorce, as to what shall be the proper causes, and in case of separation, to whom the guardianship of the children shall be given, as to be wholly regardless of the happiness of women—the law, in all cases, going upon a false supposition of the supremacy of man, and giving all power into his hands.

"After depriving her of all rights as a married woman, if single and the owner of property, he has taxed her to support a government which recognizes her only when her property can be made profitable to it.

"He has monopolized nearly all the profitable employments, and from those she is permitted to follow, she receives but a scanty remuneration. He closes against her all the avenues to wealth and distinction which he considers most honorable to himself. As a teacher of theology, medicine, or law, she is not known.

"He has denied her the facilities for obtaining a thorough education, all colleges being closed against her.

"He allows her in Church, as well as State, but a subordinate position, claiming Apostolic authority for her exclusion from the ministry and, with some exceptions, from any public participation in the affairs of the Church.

"He has created a false public sentiment by giving to the world a different code of morals for men and women, by which moral delinquencies which exclude women from society are not only tolerated but deemed of little account in man.

"He has usurped the prerogative of Jehovah himself, claiming as his right to assign for her a sphere of action, when that belongs to her conscience and to her God.

"He has endeavored, in every way that he could, to destroy her confidence in her own powers, to lessen her self-respect, and to make her willing to lead a dependent and abject life.

"Now, in view of this entire disfranchisement of one-half the people of this country, their social and religious degradation—in view of the unjust laws above mentioned and because women do feel themselves aggrieved, oppressed, and fraudulently deprived of their most sacred rights, we insist that they have immediate admission to all the rights and privileges which belong to them as citizens of the United States."

They added that they anticipated "no small amount of misconception, misrepresentation, and ridicule" to be directed at their efforts. Newspapers promptly obliged by calling them aged spinsters who could not get a man.

In the years that followed, women's rights conventions and meetings were held throughout the country. Male reaction was predictable. This editorial appeared in the New York *Herald* in 1852:

*The Woman's Rights Convention—*
*The Last Act of the Drama*

*Who are these women? What do they want? What are the motives that impel them to this course of action? The* dramatis personae *of the farce enacted at Syracuse present a curious conglomeration of both sexes. Some of them are old maids whose*

> *personal charms were never very attractive, and who have been sadly slighted by the masculine gender in general; some of them women who have been badly mated, whose own temper or their husbands' has made life anything but agreeable to them, and they are therefore down upon the whole of the opposite sex; some, having so much of the virago in their disposition that nature appears to have made a mistake in their gender—mannish women, like hens that crow; some of boundless vanity and egotism who believe that they are superior in intellectual ability to "all the world and the rest of mankind" and delight to see their speeches and addresses in print; and man shall be consigned to his proper sphere—nursing the babies, washing the dishes, mending stockings and sweeping the house.*

Though political change was to be agonizingly slow, some individual women broke barriers that had been erected against them. Elizabeth Blackwell was admitted to the medical school at Geneva College over the unanimous opposition of the faculty. She had been turned down by twenty-nine other schools. The students voted to let her in because they thought it would be amusing to see a frail female faint at the sight of blood and cadavers. She graduated first in her class in 1849.

Yet, opposition to women doctors remained so strong within the male medical profession that in 1859, the Medical Society of Philadelphia voted to "excommunicate" every doctor who taught in a medical school for women or who consulted with a woman doctor or with a man who taught women medical students.

When London University Medical School was finally opened to women in 1872, many male students protested that their "property rights had been invaded by this action," because permitting women to practice "lowered the value of their own diplomas."

Barriers to the law were even more impenetrable. Myra Bradwell appealed to the Supreme Court when she was refused permission to practice law in Illinois. The court declared that "God designed the sexes to occupy different spheres of action and that it belongs to men to make, apply and execute the laws." The good justices said that by admitting this woman, people might think they were saying that women could be judges and government officials as well, and "this we are not yet prepared to hold."

Feminist Jane Swisshelm, who published the *Pittsburgh Visitor*, had a comment about that kind of mentality. She pointed out that it was well enough for women to do "men's jobs" when they were low-paid drudgery. "They plough, harrow, reap, dig, make hay, rake, bind grain, thresh, chop wood, milk, churn, do anything that is hard work, physical labor, and who says anything against it? But," she said, "let one presume to use her mental powers—let her aspire to turn editor, public speaker, doctor, lawyer—take up any profession or avocation which is deemed honorable and requires talent, and O! bring cologne, get a cambric kerchief and feather fan, unloose his corsets and take off his cravat! What a fainting fit Mr. Propriety has taken! Just to think that 'one of the deah creatures'—the heavenly angels, should forsake the sphere—woman's sphere—to mix with the wicked strife of this wicked world!" In 1850, Jane Swisshelm succeeded in entering the House of Representatives all-male Press gallery.

Other women turned their energies to the struggle for the vote, gathering petitions, convincing legislators to introduce suffrage bills into state legislatures and the United States Congress, lobbying, speaking, holding meetings, and finally demonstrating and parading in major cities to underscore their demands.

Susan B. Anthony, a brilliant strategist and leader of the suffrage movement, devoted her life to the cause. "By law, public sentiment and religion from the time of Moses down to the present day, woman has never been thought of other than as a piece of property, to be disposed of at the will and pleasure of man," she declared. "Women must be educated out of their unthinking acceptance of financial dependence on man into mental and economic independence." She deplored the need for women to "sell themselves—in marriage or out—for bread and shelter."

And she protested against the fact that the laws that most intimately affected women—"the statutes for marriage and divorce, for adultery, breach of promise, seduction, rape, bigamy, abortion, infanticide—all were made by men. They alone decide who are guilty of violating these laws and what shall be their punishment, with judge, jury, and advocate all men, with no woman's voice heard. . . ."

One of her first political actions was to collect thousands of signatures on a suffrage petition to the New York State Legislature. The Assembly Judiciary Committee in 1856 responded with the snide comment that "the ladies always have the best place and choicest tidbit at the table. They always have the best seat in the cars, carriages and sleighs; the warmest place in the winter and the coolest place in summer. They have their choice on which side of the bed they will lie, front or back. . . . If there is any inequity or oppression in the case, the gentlemen are the sufferers."

The feminists could hardly have predicted the low level of vulgarity to which many of the nation's insensitive lawmakers and editorial writers would sink.

The suffragists scoffed bitterly at the chivalrous pretentions of the opposition. "All the generous promptings of chivalry, all the poetry of romantic gallantry, depend upon woman's retaining her place as dependent and defenceless, and making no claims and maintaining no rights but what are the rights of honor, rectitude and love," declared Angelina Grimke. "If all this sinful foolery is to be withdrawn from our sex, with all my heart I say, the sooner the better. Yea, I say more, no woman who lives up to the true glory of her womanhood will ever be treated with such practical contempt."

And Elizabeth Cady Stanton said, "Talk not to us of chivalry, that died long ago. . . . In social life, true, a man in love will jump to pick up a glove or bouquet for a silly girl of sixteen, whilst at home he will permit his aged mother to carry pails of water and armfuls of wood or his wife to lug a twenty-pound baby, hour after hour, without ever offering to relieve her."

In an article called "Losing Her Privilege," Alice Stone Blackwell, Lucy Stone's daughter, remarked, "So Bishop Vincent is reported to have said that if women were allowed to vote, he should never again offer a lady his seat in a horse-car. But the Bishop had forgotten his logic. Why does he now offer a lady his seat? Is it because she cannot vote or because she is presumably not so well able to stand as he is?" She added, "Justice is better than chivalry if we cannot have both."

Sojourner Truth, who had been born into slavery, gave perhaps the most moving rejoinder to a clergyman who protested the idea of woman's suffrage with patronizing references to woman's frailty. Her stirring declaration will live on in history.

"The man over there says women need to be helped into carriages and lifted over ditches, and to have the best places everywhere," she declared. "Nobody ever helps me into carriages or over puddles, or gives me the best place—and ain't I a woman? Look at my arm! I have ploughed and planted and gathered into barns and no man could head me—and ain't I a woman? I could work as much and eat as much as a man—when I could get it—and bear the lash as well! And ain't I a woman? I have borne thirteen children, and seen most of 'em sold into slavery, and when I cried out with my mother's grief, none but Jesus heard me—and ain't I a woman?"

A woman who was present at the meeting reported the response. "Amid roars of applause, she returned to her corner, leaving more than one of us with streaming eyes."

Women did win some legal victories even before they obtained the right to vote. Beginning with New York in 1848, some states passed married women's property laws, giving wives control over their own earnings and inheritances. One of the forces behind these laws was wealthy men who did not want their sons-in-law to fritter away the estates they passed on to their daughters.

Yet, women still lacked these rights in many states. The Legislature of Tennessee conducted a debate that concluded that women had no souls; therefore, they would not be allowed to own their own property. The plight of one woman at that time was not uncommon. She had been a successful milliner, while her husband had failed in business. When he died he left *her* property to his illegitimate children, and at sixty-two, she had to go out to work again to earn money to keep alive.

One feminist, Lucy Stone, struck a symbolic blow against the restrictions put upon women by marriage by, in 1855, signing a novel wedding contract with her husband, Henry Blackwell, who was the brother of Dr. Elizabeth Blackwell. It said in part:

*While we acknowledge our mutual affection by publicly assuming the relation of man and wife, yet in justice to ourselves and a great principle, we deem it a duty to declare that this act on our part implies no sanction of, nor promise of voluntary obedience to, such of the present laws of marriage as refuse to recognize the wife as an independent, rational being while they confer upon the husband an injurious and unnatural superiority, investing him with legal powers which no honorable man would exercise and no man should possess. We protest especially against the laws which give the husband:*

*1. The custody of the wife's person.*

*2. The exclusive control and guardianship of their children.*

*3. The sole ownership of her personal property and use of her real estate, unless previously settled upon her or placed in the hands of trustees as in the case of minors, lunatics, and idiots.*

*4. The absolute right to the product of her industry. [Her wages]*

Lucy Stone also kept her own last name, a practice which many of today's feminists are repeating. This action symbolized that she had her own identity and worth and was not merely an extension of her husband.

Lucy Stone spoke widely about the injustices of the sexist system. At a women's rights convention in Cincinnati, Ohio in 1855, she declared, "Do not tell us before we are born even that our province is to cook dinners, darn stockings, and sew on buttons. We are told women have all the rights she wants; and even women, I am ashamed to say, tell us so. They mistake the politeness of men for rights—seats while men stand in this hall tonight, and their adulations, but these are mere courtesies. We want rights. The flour-merchant, the house-builder and the postman charge us no less on account of our sex; but when we endeavor to earn money to pay all these, then, indeed we find the difference."

Later, in 1898, Charlotte Perkins Gilman called for an end to the notion that woman's chief role is as wife and mother. "The economic position of woman in the world heretofore has been that of the domestic servant. . . . Economic dependence is the underlying ground of the helplessness of women," she said. In *Woman and Economics*, she declared that women should work so that they could be independent, and she proposed communal housekeeping arrangements with a paid staff to do the cooking, cleaning, and care for the children. "How do we know that the care of children by one individual mother in the personally conducted home is the best thing for the world?" she asked.

Suffragist Amelia Bloomer made the same proposal in a speech called "Housekeeping—Woman's Burden." Antoinette Brown Blackwell, the first woman ordained as a minister and Lucy Stone's sister-in-law, proposed that "wife and husband could be mutual helpers with admirable effect. Let her take his place in garden or field or workshop an hour or two daily, learning to breathe more strongly and exercising a fresh set of muscles in soul and body. To him baby-tending and bread-making would be most humanizing in their influence.

"Let no women give all their time to household duties, but require nearly all women and all men also, since they belong to the household, to bear some share of the common household burdens."

During the Civil War, the question of women's rights was pushed aside and many of the suffragists—who had been active in the abolition cause all along—devoted themselves solely to the struggle against slavery. Several hundred women disguised themselves as men and fought alongside other soldiers solidly proving the fiction of feminine frailty. Harriet Tubman, an ex-slave who had risked her life to guide more than 300 slaves to safety on the Underground Railroad, organized a spy and scouting corps for the General Staff's Intelligence Service in the Union Army.

When the war was over and Congress began to frame the constitutional amendments that would give freed slaves the rights of citizens, the suffragists were outraged to learn that the legislators had no intention of extending those rights to black women—or to white women, for that matter. The Fourteenth Amendment wrote "male" into the Constitution for the first time.

Abolitionist Horace Greeley stated in his *New York Tribune:* "Talk of a true woman needing the ballot as an accessory of power when she rules the world with the glance of an eye." He said that "the best women" he knew did not want to vote. His own wife disagreed quite strongly and presented a petition for woman suffrage to the New York State Legislature.

The women felt sold out. They had worked hard in the abolitionist cause, and now their male colleagues told them to wait, that "this was the Negro's hour." The Negro *man's* hour, they could have added. And they waited—for another fifty-two years.

These suffragists did, however, have male friends who were both philosophic and political supporters of the movement. In 1869, John Stuart Mill wrote "On the Subjection of Women." He said, "Women are declared to be better than men, an empty compliment which must provoke a bitter smile from every woman of spirit since there is no other situation in life in which it is the established order and quite natural and suitable that the better obey the worse." (Mill was jailed for his advocacy of contraception.)

The year before, Senator S. C. Pomeroy of Kansas had introduced the first women's suffrage bill into Congress. Other bills were proposed in individual state legislatures. In the years that followed, women like Susan B. Anthony, Elizabeth Cady Stanton, Lucy Stone, Carrie Chapman Catt, Alice Paul, and countless thousands of others, devoted themselves to winning the right to vote.

They canvassed and lobbied and gave speeches in virtually every city and town in the country. Often they were heckled; sometimes opponents hired thugs to break up their meetings; they were pelted with stones and eggs and, in church meetings, even Bibles. Someone turned an icy hose on Lucy Stone in mid winter, but she pulled her shawl tight around her and went right on speaking.

Lucy Stone and others refused to pay their taxes on the grounds that it was taxation without representation, and the government seized their property and sold it. Some who did not withhold their taxes attached messages of protest to the payments.

Part of the opposition to women's suffrage came from men who accepted the traditional notions about women's place and inferiority. However, clandestine financial opposition came from the liquor interests, which feared women would vote for prohibition, and from railroad and manufacturing interests who feared any change that would threaten their control of political officials. In 1918, a congressional committee accidentally turned up evidence of the activities of these groups when it was investigating the relationship between the liquor interests and the Germans during World War I. Ironically, the prohibition amendment was passed before women got the vote, and it was repealed afterward!

Suffrage came earliest in the West, where women who plowed, hunted, and chopped wood beside the men made the idea of women's inferiority seem ridiculous. Women first voted in the territory of Wyoming in 1869. When Congress wanted to detain Wyoming's admission to the Union until it ended women's suffrage, the legislature wired back: "We will remain out of the Union a hundred years rather than come in without the women." They were admitted.

When Susan B. Anthony and fifteen other women insisted on casting ballots in the election of 1872, she was arrested on the grounds that she "knowingly, wrongfully, and unlawfully voted for a representative to the Congress of the United States." One newspaper charged that such "female lawlessness" proved that women were not fit to vote. Other editorial writers expressed overbearing concern that women voters would be forced to mix with uncouth elements at the polls. "No real lady would want to vote," they said. "Besides," they added, "allowing women to vote would destroy marriage and the home." Some women agreed, though in the same year, Victoria Woodhull became the first woman to be nominated for President when she was chosen to carry the banner of the National Equal Rights Party.

The judge in the voting case refused to allow Susan B. Anthony to testify in her own defense; he said she was "incompetent"—and she was fined $100. She was almost superhuman in her tireless dedication. In one year, she traveled 13,000 miles and gave 108 speeches for the cause of women's suffrage. But success came slowly.

Oklahoma legislators put women in the same category as idiots, children, and criminals when it drew up its state constitution in 1904. The vote was denied to those who were illiterate, minors, mentally incompetent, convicted of a serious crime—or women!

Clothing workers organizer Rose Schneidermann lashed out at the condescending opinion that the right to vote would make women lose their "femininity." "We have women working in the foundries, stripped to the waist, if you please, because of the heat." She noted dryly, "Surely these women won't lose any more of their beauty and charm by putting a ballot in a ballot box once a year than they are likely to lose standing in foundries or laundries all year round."

Clergymen were often in the forefront of the fight against suffrage, dredging up quotations from the Bible to prove that the natural order of things was female obedience to man. So, Elizabeth Cady Stanton proceeded to write a commentary on these ancient passages in the form of a book called *The Woman's Bible.*

She attacked sections of the Bible from Abraham to Joseph for providing "the lowest possible idea of womanhood, having no hope nor ambition beyond conjugal unions with men they scarcely knew. . . . There is no mention of women except when the advent of sons is announced."

"The fifth commandment will take the reader by surprise," she said. "It is rather remarkable that the young Hebrews should have been told to honor their mothers when the whole drift of the teaching thus far has been to throw contempt on the whole sex. In what way could they show their mothers honor? All the laws and customs forbid it."

Another comment came later from Catharine Waugh McCulloch, a Justice of the Peace in Illinois who was the first woman elected to judicial office in the United States. She noted that "creation was in the ascending scale, first the lower creatures, then the higher animals, then man, and last, at the apex, the more complex woman. The order of creation affords no argument why women should obey men," she declared wryly. "It might rather be a reason why men should obey women."

Alice Duer Miller was another suffragist who expressed her sentiments in a light vein. This verse, entitled "Lines to Mr. Bowdle of Ohio," was written in 1915.

*You, who despise the so-called fairer sex,*
*Be brave. There really isn't any reason*
*You should not, if you wish, oppose and vex*
*And scold us in, and even out of season;*
*But don't regard it as your bounden duty*
*To open with a tribute to our beauty.*

*Say, if you like that women have no sense,*
*No self-control, no power of concentration;*
*Say that hysterics is our one defense*
*Our virtue but an absence of temptation;*

*These I can bear, but, oh, I own it rankles*
*To hear you maundering on about our ankles.*

*Tell those old stories, which have now and then*
*Been from the Record thoughtfully deleted,*
*Repeat that favorite one about the hen,*
*Repeat the ones that cannot be repeated;*
*But in the midst of such enjoyments, smother*
*The impulse to extol your "sainted mother."*

While the suffrage battle was going on in the United States, a similar effort was being waged in England, as well as in other countries of the world. The British struggle was more violent than the American. Women broke windows, poured acid into mailboxes, and attacked members of Parliament with whips, stones, or their bare hands. When they were jailed, they conducted hunger strikes and were force-fed, a brutal procedure that requires pushing tubes deep into the throat and nasal passages.

American suffragist Alice Paul took part in those demonstrations and in the hunger strikes, so that by the time she returned to the United States, she was schooled in a new method of political action. In 1913, tens of thousands of suffragists marched in torchlight parades for women's suffrage in New York, Chicago, Boston, and Washington, D.C. In Washington, as 8,000 marchers approached the White House on Pennsylvania Avenue, unruly mobs attacked them while the police stood by and did nothing. The mobs knocked the women to the ground, slapped them and threw burning cigar stubs at them—all accompanied by appropriate curses and obscenities. Beaten and bloodied, women were rushed to the surrounding hospitals and the rioters were finally stopped by the United States Cavalry. Not one man was arrested, but after a Congressional investigation, the police chief in charge of the force was fired.

During these years, when women picketed and demonstrated they faced being attacked by the mobs and arrested by the police. In the beginning they were jailed for only a few days, but the sentences eventually grew to weeks and months. In one year, over 200 women were arrested in Washington and 97 were sent to the city jail or the Occoquan Workhouse in Virginia. Many were beaten and mistreated by guards, and when they protested with hunger strikes, they were force-fed.

Yet, their actions hardly affected the opinions of much of the opposition. Even as late as 1915, just four years before the amendment extending the franchise to women was finally passed, the *New York Times* said in an editorial that, "The grant of suffrage to women is repugnant to instincts that strike their roots deep in the order of nature. It runs counter to human reason, it flouts the teachings of experience and the admonitions of common sense."

Nevertheless, in spite of the hostility and ridicule they encountered wherever they went, the women's suffrage movement was winning adherents. The organizations formed to work for the vote had about 2 million members throughout the country, and they spent their time lobbying with Congressmen and working for candidates who promised to support the women's suffrage. First the amendment had died year after year in committee; then, when it was finally brought to a vote on the floor, it was voted down. Once the amendment was rejected by the Senate after it had passed the House. The votes were so dramatic, that once, a man who had broken his shoulder in a fall on the ice was brought in on a stretcher. Another man left his wife on her deathbed to cast his ballot the way she had wanted—for women's suffrage.

Finally, the years of grueling work paid off. In 1919, both houses of Congress passed an amendment giving women the right to vote. It took fourteen months more to win ratification by three-fourths of the states—thirty-six at that time. The vote in the last state, Tennessee, was a repeat of the drama as liquor interests and others in the antisuffrage lobby sought to bribe and threaten the members of the legislature. The amendment was ratified with the vote of Harry Burn—at twenty-four, the youngest member of the Legislature—who had been uncertain of how to cast his ballot until he received a message from his mother who wrote: "I have been watching to see how you stood, but have not noticed anything yet." She urged him to "be a good boy" and vote for suffrage. He did.

The Nineteenth Amendment to the United States Constitution was signed by Secretary of State Brainbridge Colby on August 26, 1920, giving 26 million women equal rights in choosing the officials and influencing the policies of their government. Later, looking back at what had been accomplished, Suffragist Carrie Chapman Catt wrote: "To get that word, 'male,' out of the Constitution, cost the women of this country 52 years of pauseless campaigns; 56 state referendum campaigns; 480 legislative campaigns to get state amendments submitted, 47 state constitutional convention campaigns, 277 state party convention campaigns, 19 campaigns to get suffrage planks in the party platforms, 19 campaigns with 19 successive Congresses to get the federal amendment submitted, and the final ratification campaign."

Even then, the opposition would not rest, and for two years they fought the amendment in the courts. Finally, in 1922, the Supreme Court ruled that women could indeed vote in the United States of America.

Meanwhile, the battle was going on in other parts of the world. Carrie Chapman Catt had helped to organize the International Woman Suffrage Alliance in 1904. Between then and 1920, women had won the vote in twenty-two countries.

Somehow, in the United States and other countries where women voted, the dire predictions of the male supremicists did not come true. Women did not become "coarse" and "unfeminine," and they did not leave their husbands or stop having children. Unfortunately, they did not take an equal place with men in government either. The country may have been ready to give women the vote, but they were not about to elect women to public office or allow them into the political parties—except as envelope stuffers and tea party fund raisers.

And most of the suffragist leaders themselves seemed content to retire to their homes and let the substance of their victory slip from their fingers. The major suffrage organization turned into the League of Women Voters, which lobbies for legislation and educates women about government, but does not take part in electoral politics. Women were active in lobbying for reform legislation—for child labor laws and pure food and drug statues—but it was to be nearly fifty years before the familiar phrases and demands of feminism were to be heard again in America.

# CHAPTER FOURTEEN WOMEN AND SEX

The questions of abortion and contraception are closely tied to the attitude that men have traditionally held about women as people and sexual beings. Our society lives with a remnant of a double standard once so severe that in the 1700's, women who committed adultery were stoned or burned to death while their lovers went free; in the 1800's, unwed mothers were cast out from society while people murmured a few words about "sowing wild oats" to unwed fathers; and society still looks askance at women who enjoy sex without marriage, though men who would abstain from it are considered abnormal.

Some societies thought women altogether too inferior to be sexual partners. Here is one contemporary explanation of Greek homosexuality: "Let marriage be for all, but let the love of boys remain alone the privilege of the wise, for perfect virtue is unthinkable in women."

We have already seen that the early Christians believed that sex was bad for everyone, and this hatred and disgust of sexuality have filtered down through the centuries and persisted, even if only unconsciously, in our society, where people have been made to believe that sex is evil and dirty. There has been an even greater prohibition of sex outside marriage.

In about 70 percent of societies, premarital sex has been permitted.

In the rest it has been forbidden (mostly to women) either to avoid the birth of children outside of marriage or because there was a premium on virgin brides. The Book of Deuteronomy in the Bible states that if "the tokens of virginity be not found for the damsel, then they shall bring out the damsel to the door of her father's house and the men of the city shall stone her with stones that she die."

Throughout history, there has always been a double sex standard imposed on men and women. Some of it had to do with the idea that women were property, and nonvirgins were akin to "used" merchandise. If a woman committed adultery she could be punished severely, but nothing would happen to her husband if he had an extramarital affair.

In ancient Greece and Rome, and among the Muslims, men could be unfaithful to their wives, but women who committed adultery were guilty of a crime. Among the ancient Hebrews, a young bride could be stoned to death if the village elders agreed with her husband's charge that she was not a virgin. And if a man slept with an engaged woman, both of them would be put to death—the man because he had violated another man's rights.

In Anglo-Saxon Britain from the fifth through the eleventh centuries, women charged with adultery were strangled and burned. Again, there was no such penalty for adulterous husbands. However, the men who were the lovers of these women were punished like other thieves—depending on the amount of money originally paid to buy the wife.

In the late 1600's, Lord Halifax instructed women on the subject of adultery: "Remember, that next to the danger of committing the fault yourself, the greatest is that of seeing it in your husband." He assured them that "your discretion and silence will be the most prevailing reproof."

In colonial America, a single woman who had a child might have been whipped, fined, or put in jail even if everyone knew that she had been seduced. Fathers went unpunished, though they might be ordered to help support their children.

Until recently, women who had sex outside of marriage kept it a shameful secret while men bragged about all the lovers they had had and at the same time condemned the very women they had slept with as "loose" and "immoral."

After a while society stopped saying sex was wrong. It just insisted that sex was something that "nice women" should not be interested in. In fact, a British gynecologist named William Acton wrote in the 1800's that it was a "vile aspersion" to intimate that any normal woman had any desire for sex.

Doctors at that time performed clitoridectomies on women—they removed or cauterized the clitoris, the center of female sexual pleasure, because they believed that sexual excitement was responsible for "hysteria" (from the Greek *hystericus*, which means "of the womb") and other mental illness in women.

This attitude toward sex was not the case in many societies such as the Samoan where sex is looked upon as an art and a form of recreation, nor was it always true in Western civilization. Nevertheless, it resulted in a situation where sex was a service or duty that women performed either for the enjoyment of men—or as a means of becoming pregnant.

Men enjoyed sex all along—with wives or with young girls they seduced or with prostitutes they bought with their pocket money.

Saint Jerome did not believe in the double standard: "It cannot be that an adulterous wife should be put away and an unfaithful husband retained," but not many seem to have paid any attention to him.

Some societies think sex is natural, others think it is improper outside of marriage. This can be accepted, but what is hard to comprehend is the notion that extramarital sex should be permitted for men but not for women. After all, with whom are the men going to have sex? As a result of the double standard, several things have happened. First, men have caused women to develop irrational inhibitions and fears about sex, often making it impossible for them to enjoy it even when married. It is hard for them to get rid of the idea that sex is something dirty and evil when they have been warned against it from the time they were children.

Second, they created an oppressed and brutalized class of women who have been the prostitutes, concubines, harem slaves, and streetwalkers of civilization. While men piously declaimed about the purity of women—and refused to let them participate in the "ugly" world of commerce—they drove impoverished women into the streets to sell their bodies to earn enough to live.

For centuries, methods of contraception and abortion were primitive and not very effective. (Old Egyptian papyruses show that contraception was used there in 1900 B.C.) But women were denied even these remedies for unwanted pregnancies. Male moralists declared that the "wicked sinners" had to be punished for their evil doings (having children was thus a punishment—not a very likely beginning for any new baby).

Because the only socially justifiable reason for sex was children, even wives were forced to undergo one pregnancy after another until women in their thirties were drudges—haggard and drawn from bearing children and caring for them. It was hardly unusual to have eight or nine—and to bury several more that died in their infancy. (And people ask why history has not produced many great women in the arts or sciences! There has always been a reverse relationship between the birth rate and the status of women.)

As a result of their inability to avoid having children, many women (and their husbands) committed infanticide. In the late eighteenth and nineteenth centuries in Europe, thousands of infants died of starvation, suffocation, or poisoning. Others were left in foundling homes—a kind of infanticide too, for there many died of malnutrition or neglect.

Between 1817 and 1820 in France, 36 percent of all the children born were abandoned—a total of several hundred thousand. Napoleon ordered that turntable devices be set up at foundling hospitals so that parents could leave their infants there without being seen or made to answer embarrassing questions. Finally, in the middle of the 1800's, French biologists discovered the role that the male sperm played in fertilizing the female ovum and devised the condom—called "the French letter." The birth rate was cut in half.

Yet, public opinion was hardly favorable to contraception. In 1822, a men's-store owner named Francis Place printed leaflets addressed "To the Married of Both Sexes of the Working People," advising them to use a sponge tied to a ribbon and inserted into the women to prevent conception. Many of his friends stopped talking to him.

Some fifty-five years later, a British feminist named Annie Besant was arrested for publishing a pamphlet on birth control. The jury ruled that the book was "calculated to deprave public morals," and people assailed her as "unwomanly" for even testifying in her own behalf in court.

Doctors were hardly helpful in the fight. In 1888, Dr. Isaac Pierce, discussing contraception, declared, "It is true we may prevent criminal abortion, we may lessen suffering, pauperism, and neglect among children," *but*, he charged, it would promote "immorality."

The prime fighter against "immorality" in the United States was Anthony Comstock, who founded the New York Society for the Suppression of Vice in 1873. (Its president was soap manufacturer Samuel Colgate.) Comstock got Congress to pass a law making it illegal to send obscene literature through the mails or to transport it from one state to another—and contraceptives or information about them were on his obscenity list.

Of course, exceptions were made for the benefit of men. In New York State, the law allowed contraception for the cure or prevention of disease, but this was interpreted only to refer to the use of condoms, the male contraceptives, to prevent venereal disease in men. Doctors could not give birth-control devices to women even if their lives would be endangered by pregnancy.

That law was in effect for forty-two years and was the reason for hundreds of jail sentences. Comstock, who was responsible for enforcing the law, once even raided a leading art school which had published some studies of nudes in its magazine. He banned from the mails a magazine called "The Cradle" which advocated chastity for both men and women. Comstock said the subject was unfit for discussion. A man who fought against Comstock, Moses Harman, was sentenced to five years in jail at the age of fifty-nine for writing an article which protested an incident in which a man had sexually assaulted his wife while she was recovering from a serious operation.

Margaret Sanger spent time in jail, too, before she won her fight to make birth control legal. However, until 1969 it was illegal to dispense birth-control supplies to anyone in the state of Connecticut, and until 1970 they were not permitted to be given to unmarried persons in Massachusetts. It is still generally illegal to give contraceptive information or devices to girls under sixteen. Unfortunately, there is no way to pass a law to prevent thirteen-, fourteen-, and fifteen-year-olds from getting pregnant, and thousands are forced to drop out of school and suffer untold mental anguish from pregnancies each year. Those who believe that sex is evil might think that these girls are getting their just "punishment."

# CHAPTER FIFTEEN PRELUDE TO THE NEW FEMINISM

In the years after the passage of the Nineteenth Amendment, women did not take their places alongside men in the halls of Congress or on the boards of directors of corporations, but they did move out into the world in greater numbers. Their increased entrance into the labor force was due more to World War I than any legislation—with men in the army, women were needed to manufacture airplanes, armaments, and the uniforms the soldiers wore, and they replaced men at certain jobs, producing the goods and services that supplied the population.

By 1920, when one in five workers was female, the average working woman was twenty-eight years old, single, and most likely to be a factory worker. Large numbers of women worked as clerks, maids, and on farms, and less than one out of four worked at all. As the years went on, increasing numbers of women went on to higher education. They had earned under 20 percent of all bachelors' degrees in 1900, but by 1930 they had more than doubled that percentage. In the same year, nearly 33 percent of college professors were women. Of course, the depression cut off opportunities for everyone as both male and female unemployment rates soared.

Yet, employers sought to take advantage of the age-old discrimination. Women were fired and replaced by men—or if they were hired or kept on, it was at reduced wages. Some people argued that married women had no right to hold jobs at all since they were said to be taking jobs away from men. No one mentioned that many of them were either supporting their families when husbands with different skills could not find work (firing a woman who worked in a shop would hardly help her husband who was a carpenter)—or that without two salaries, their families might starve. Some legislators actually proposed laws to prevent married women from working.

Then came the rise of Hitler and the beginning of a national mobilization for the expected war. That spelled the end of the depression. By 1940, women comprised over 40 percent of college graduates and held 45 percent of all professional and technical jobs—although most of these jobs were as teachers or nurses. When the United States entered the war at the end of 1941, suddenly there was not only full employment, there was a scarcity of workers. Women were told that it was their patriotic duty to work in the munitions factories and at other jobs that had been left vacant by the soldiers. And with the men off to war, many women found it necessary to work to support themselves and their families. "Rosie the Riveter" became a national symbol, as women became welders, machinists, and truck drivers, or took other jobs that had always been considered "men's work."

However, women found that although they were permitted to do the work of men, often they were not given men's pay. Michigan and Montana had enacted equal pay laws in 1919—but no other states followed suit for almost twenty-five years. During the war, equal pay laws were passed in Illinois, Massachusetts, New York, and Washington. By 1950, six other states had approved similar legislation; by 1955, four more were added to the list. The laws did away with some of the most blatant forms of discrimination, but by and large, men continued to earn more than women for doing the same work. In 1957, the median income of women was about $3,000 compared to $4,700 for men, though some of the difference was due to the concentration of women in jobs that paid less to everyone.

An equal pay for women act was introduced into Congress by Representative Helen Gahagan Douglas in 1945, but it failed. It was proposed at every session for the next eighteen years, but it did not gain a majority until 1963—and even then, the law that was passed excluded women in professional, executive, and administrative jobs from coverage.

During the war, Congress passed the Lanham Act which set up day-care centers for the children of mothers who worked in defense plants. Three million women had been brought into the war industries. (And another 266,000 joined the armed forces.) But when the war was over almost all the centers were closed. Women were told that their place was "in the home," and a period of reaction set in.

Some of them went home, but too many had seen the advantages of bringing in their own paychecks. In 1940, only 33 percent of women workers were married; by 1950, wives made up 50 percent of the female labor force. However, America's socio-cultural propaganda machine geared up to tell them that they were shortchanging their husbands, ruining their children, and acting out their own deep-seated desires to be men. This was the era of the "feminine mystique," when the image of the truly desirable woman was a "Little Miss Housewife" with a starched white apron, getting the children off to dancing school and batting practice and standing behind a white picket fence in the suburbs to welcome hubby home from the office when he arrived on the 5:15 train.

Women's magazines that had written about the exciting lives of wartime career girls now turned to clucking their tongues about the poor, brassy female who didn't understand that her true happiness lay in bending over a bassinet or creating exotic meals from hamburger. (Nobody asked why the women writers and editors who gave the advice were not doing the same. And some of the architects of the "feminine mystique" were men.)

Many women either believed what they read or genuinely preferred taking care of their own families to being "office wives" and catering to male administrators and executives or working on factory production lines. There had been about 13.7 million women workers before the war, there were over 19 million on the job during the war, and only 16 million when the conflict was over. Yet, that was still an increase; over 2 million did not buy the "feminine mystique." They had found work interesting—or at least profitable—and in the years to follow the percentage of working women climbed higher until nearly 20 million were working by the mid-nineteen-fifties. More than one out of every three women was working, and they made up nearly 33 percent of the country's labor force.

Having children no longer seemed to be as much of a barrier against working as in the past because women who had put their children in child-care centers to enable them to work in war plants found out that it did not make their youngsters feel unloved or turn them into raging neurotics. Under 9 percent of mothers had worked in 1940, but after the war, over 18 percent had jobs. The figures spiraled so that by the mid-fifties, over 27 percent were working—and that included 18 percent of mothers with children under six. The numbers rose sharply when the children reached school age and the women no longer had day-care problems.

Most of the women were employed as clerical, factory, and service workers. Between 1940 and 1950, there was actually a decrease in the percentage of women professional and technical workers. In 1940, women had earned over 40 percent of all college degrees; this percentage had fallen to under 24 percent a decade later.

In the decade before the rise of the new feminist movement in the mid 1960's, there was little improvement made in the position of women in society—in fact, though women made breakthroughs into some jobs, the salary gap between men and women actually widened. Congress had passed an Equal Pay Act in 1963, but it seemed to do little good. Whereas in 1955, women were likely to earn about sixty-four cents for every dollar a man received, by 1965 it was down to sixty cents. By that year, women were both a smaller percentage of college graduates and held a substantially smaller share of the college teaching and professional jobs than in 1940.

Most women still worked in low-paid occupations—about 5 million as clerical workers, nearly 3 million as sales, service, and domestic workers, and another 2.3 million as factory workers.

Increasing numbers of women were working—nearly 45 percent by 1965. By that year about 35 percent of all mothers had jobs, including 25 percent of the women with preschool children. However, child-care facilities were virtually nonexistent.

Women had won the vote, but that did not turn out to mean that they had gained political equality. In the years after 1916, when

Jeanette Rankin of Montana became the first woman elected to Congress, only a handful of women served in the House or the Senate. In 1947–48, for example, there were eight women Representatives and no Senators in Congress. By 1955–56, female representation had only reached the unimpressive number of one Senator and sixteen Representatives. Women who joined political parties soon discovered that they were expected to stuff envelopes, hold fund raising parties, and stay out of the meetings where policy decisions were made and candidates for office chosen. To make sure that women would not intrude, separate women's divisions were set up and the women who joined them found that they had virtually nothing to do with party politics.

By 1965, there were two women Senators out of a total of 100, but the number of women in the House was down to 10. And in the states, women held only 370 of the more than 7,800 seats in the legislatures—under 5 percent. South Carolina had no women in either house, and in 25 other states, one branch of the legislature was as stag as a men's locker room. New Hampshire, Vermont, and Connecticut had the most women representatives, with 68, 47, and 48 respectively—about 44 percent of the national total.

In the area of education, magazine writers and others suggested that there ought to be limits set on women's admissions to colleges—and that they should even be barred from higher education to make sure that all the men who wished to enroll could find places.

Women faced many kinds of special discrimination. Often, they were fired when employers discovered that they were pregnant, or they were denied maternity leave and the right to return to their jobs. Though men with company life or medical insurance policies could claim their wives as dependents, women could not claim their husbands. There were often separate seniority lists for men and women in factories; women were refused promotions on the grounds that men would not like taking orders from them, and in some cases, women—but not men—were forbidden to smoke on the job. (By and large these conditions still exist.)

Even in the so-called "women's professions," women were losing ground. Men began moving into public education—and into jobs as principals and school superintendents that at least a few women had held in the past. They became the directors of social work programs and the heads of large city library systems. In 1965, the Navy, for the first time admitted six women to apprenticeship programs as aircraft instrument mechanics, sailmakers, coppersmiths, metalsmiths, and patternmakers, but the entrance into such "male" professions in government and private industry hardly made up for the loss of other job opportunities. The biggest increase of female employment was in the service industries (hairdresser, waitress, etc.).

But 1965 was also the year that a landmark piece of legislation went into effect that was to provide the impetus for a dramatic challenge to the status of women in this country, not only in employment, but in every area of American life.

The proposed Civil Rights Act of 1964 had included a section that was aimed at ending job discrimination against blacks and other minorities. However, one Sunday afternoon, House Rules Committee Chairman Howard W. Smith of Virginia was confronted on a television interview show by journalist May Craig who had made a habit of asking government officials and legislators what they were doing for women.

She asked Representative Smith if he would amend the bill to give protection to women, and Smith, who saw this as a way to hurt the bill's chances of passage, replied that he just might do that. He also thought it would be a pretty good joke—imagine, equal job rights for women! Emanuel Celler, the Democratic sponsor of the bill, promptly rose in opposition, asking his colleagues to think of what the amendment would do to "traditional family relationships."

While many "liberal" male representatives fought the bill, all but one of the women supported it—and miraculously, it passed.

A year later, Representative Edith Green introduced a bill to repeal an 1870 law that gave federal appointing officers the right to consider only men for government jobs. It had become the general practice to request only men for all high posts. The United States Attorney General had ruled this improper in 1962, but the Green bill made it impossible for any future administration to change its mind.

A third of all federal workers were women, but they were concentrated in the lower-paying clerical positions and women were only 5 percent of the more than 150,000 senior level officials. Women protested that they had not come very far since 1883, when the first civil service exam was given. A woman received the highest score that year—but she got the second appointment!

In 1965, President Lyndon Johnson had issued an Executive Order banning job discrimination by federal contractors against racial or ethnic minorities. Two years later, he extended that order to cover women, although it did not go into effect for another year.

The battle for equality in employment was not quite over after the passage of these laws and orders—in fact, it was hardly begun. The Equal Employment Opportunity Commission, which was set up to enforce Title VII of the Civil Rights Act (the section on job discrimination), had no intention of taking the problem of sex discrimination seriously. Aileen Hernandez, the first woman member of the EEOC, resigned in protest and disgust at its inaction.

Furthermore, the EEOC had no real enforcement powers. All it could do was attempt to "conciliate" the dispute and give the person making a complaint the right to go to court to sue for the job or promotion or salary she deserved. That took lawyers, and lawyers cost money. It wasn't a route most women took easily, especially since they had to sign their names to the complaints and were liable to be harassed or fired from their jobs.

It is at this point that the most recent history of the status and struggle of women becomes intertwined with the story of the rise of the second wave of feminism—the new women's liberation movement.

*"They alone whose souls are fired through personal experience and suffering can set forth the height and depth, the source and center of the degradation of women . . . The mass of women are developed at least to the point of discontent, and that, in the dawn of this nation, was considered a most dangerous point in the British Parliament and is now deemed equally so on a Southern plantation. In the human soul, the steps between discontent and action are few and short indeed."*

*Elizabeth Cady Stanton, 1855*

# CHAPTER SIXTEEN THE MOVEMENT IS BORN AGAIN

On August 26, 1970, thousands of women in dozens of cities across the country joined in parades, demonstrations, meetings, and symbolic actions to celebrate the fiftieth anniversary of the day women won the right to vote—the day that President Woodrow Wilson's Secretary of State signed the Nineteenth Amendment into law.

In New York they set up a child-care center in City Hall Park to dramatize the need for universal day care. In Boston they handed out cans of contraceptive foam to protest laws that restricted the availability of birth control supplies. In Chicago, they held sit-ins at restaurants that barred women. In San Francisco and Los Angeles, they took over radio stations (with the approval of the management) and devoted the day to talk of women's liberation. In Washington, D.C., they lobbied with senators to urge passage of an Equal Rights Amendment for women. And in Rochester, New York, they staged a mock tea party at the home of Susan B. Anthony—and then smashed their tea cups to symbolize the end of women's traditional role in politics.

Some of the slogans of the protest day were humorous: "Don't Iron While the Strike Is Hot!" "Don't Cook Dinner—Starve a Rat Today!" and "Eve Was Framed!" But the chief slogans and aims of the National Women's Strike for Equality focused on needs that were felt by women across the country and on demands that they had been making for decades. They were for complete equality in employment and education, free twenty-four-hour child-care centers, free abortions for all women who want them, and passage of the Equal Rights Amendment to the United States Constitution.

The August 26 demonstration was seen by many as the turning point in the growth of the new feminism. It was dramatic proof that women's liberation had indeed begun to develop into a mass movement; and some political leaders began to recognize, if they had not done so before, that they had better take the demands of the movement seriously.

Actually, there had been rumblings of some official concern about the condition of women in 1961, when President John F. Kennedy established a Commission on the Status of Women. The Women's Bureau of the Labor Department had existed since 1920, but it had little power or prestige and was largely a research and information organization. The members of the President's Commission considered not only the woman's role in private and federal employment, but also her status in politics, education, law, and the need for expanded child-care facilities.

In 1963, the year that his Commission presented its report, President Kennedy set up an Interdepartmental Committee on the Status of Women that included cabinet chiefs and heads of important departments, and a Citizens Advisory Council on the Status of Women with members drawn from business, professional, and voluntary groups. The Committee was to evaluate the government's own progress in advancing the status of women; the Council was to promote action through private institutions. The Executive Director of both groups was Catherine East, who was committed to the cause of women's rights.

Within a year or two, governors in forty-four states had appointed their own commissions to study the needs of women, and they also held meetings and issued reports. (By February, 1967, all fifty states had commissions.)

Some of the women who had become involved in these commissions soon began to feel that they would be buried in a sea of reports and resolutions, exhausted by study groups and conferences, and still see little or no advancement in their cause. The last straw proved to be a meeting of the Governors' Commissions in June, 1966, in Washington, D.C.

One of the participants in the conference was Betty Friedan who had written a book called *The Feminine Mystique.* It recounted the unhappiness of educated women who gave up their careers to become suburban housewives and it received national attention when it was published in 1963. She was at the conference to attempt to organize a group that would take action on women's rights.

At first, some of the women at the meeting insisted that a new organization was not necessary. They changed their minds a day later when Dr. Kathryn Clarenbach, head of the Wisconsin Commission, was not allowed by the conference organizers to introduce a resolution against the Equal Employment Opportunity Commission's allowance of sex-segregated newspaper help-wanted ads.

An organizing conference for the National Organization for Women (NOW) was held in October. Betty Friedan became NOW's first president and Dr. Clarenbach was named chairman of the board. When their terms expired, their places were taken by Aileen Hernandez, who had been the first woman commissioner on the EEOC, and by Wilma Scott Heide, a member of the Pennsylvania Human Relations Commission. NOW continues to be the only women's rights organization of its kind organized on a national basis.

At its founding meeting, NOW adopted a statement of purpose that committed the organization to working for "true equality for all women in America and toward a fully equal partnership of the sexes as part of the worldwide revolution of human rights now taking place within and beyond our national borders."

The resolution said the time for conferences was over—now was the time to fight discrimination against women in government, industry, the professions, the churches, the political parties, the judiciary, the labor unions, education, and in every other field of importance in American life. It declared that technology had cut down the tasks women had to do in the home, and made muscular strength unnecessary in most jobs. It said, "We do not accept the traditional assumption that a woman has to choose between marriage and motherhood, on the one hand, and serious participation in industry or the professions on the other."

The convention rejected the idea that it was a man's responsibility alone to support his wife and family and called for men and women to share the responsibilities of home, family, and earning a living.

The resolution also called for political representation of women on every level of government, pledged to work for candidates who supported equal rights for women, and promised to oppose those who stood against them.

In the months and years that followed, NOW chapters were organized in cities throughout the country—slowly at first, then one after another in a spurt that seemed to begin early in 1970. By the end of that year there were one hundred chapters established or being organized from Seattle, Washington, to Baton Rouge, Louisiana. On national and local levels, NOW members fought for enforcement of Title VII by the EEOC, lobbied for the repeal of restrictive abortion laws, staged protests against restaurants that refused to serve women, fought for state laws against sex discrimination in employment, housing and education, and tried to rally support for twenty-four-hour universal child care.

The National Organization for Women also used legal means to battle discrimination. It filed a complaint against newspapers that segregated their classified job columns by sex and won a favorable decision by the EEOC, only to be forced into the courts when the American Newspaper Publishers Association ordered its lawyers to appeal that decision. Repeated picketing of *The New York Times* won a city-wide ruling against the male and female columns, and the change in newspaper policies there was followed by battles—and victories—elsewhere.

NOW attorneys Sylvia Roberts and Marguerite Rawalt filed an appeal in the case of Lorena Weeks, who had worked as a clerk for the Southern Bell Telephone Company for nineteen years and earned $78 a week. She had been turned down for the job of switchman, which paid $135 a week. The company had cited Georgia's weight-lifting law as its excuse (the "weight" was a thirty-four-pound fire extinguisher that had to be lifted in case of fire!), but when the state repealed the law in the time between the district court decision and the appeal, the company then claimed the job would require emergency work after midnight.

The court ruled in Lorena Weeks's favor in 1969, noting that other women employees were subject to work after midnight in emergencies, and declared: "Moreover, Title VII rejects just this type of romantic paternalism as unduly Victorian and instead vests individual women with the power to decide whether or not to take on unromantic tasks. Men have always had the right to determine whether the incremental increase in remuneration for strenuous, dangerous, obnoxious, boring, or unromantic tasks is worth the candle. The promise of Title VII is that women are now to be on equal footing."

That statement was a far cry from the United States Supreme Court decision in 1872 that upheld a state law barring women from the practice of law in Illinois. It said then:

"Man is or should be woman's protector and defender. The natural and proper timidity and delicacy which belongs to the female sex evidently unfits it for many of the occupations of civil life."

The high court had similarly "protected" women in 1924 when it upheld a New York State law barring the employment of women in restaurants after 10 P.M. The law made exceptions for cigarette and flower girls, ladies' rest room attendants, hotel elevator operators and charwomen—all women in lower-paying jobs that men were not so interested in "protecting" women from taking.

And, in 1948, it had upheld a Michigan statute that refused bartenders' licenses to women unless they were the wives or daughters of male bar owners. The daughters of *female* bar owners—or the female owners themselves could not get licenses! The court's reasoning was that "bartending by women may, in the allowable legislative judgment, give rise to moral and social problems." The court did not bother to give an instance of moral decay in states where women were allowed to tend bar!

One of NOW's most important battles was against the United States Labor Department which, it discovered, was not enforcing Executive Order 11246 against discrimination by companies with government contracts—an order NOW had originally pressured President Johnson to amend to include women. Women's rights advocates had been heartened by the 1967 order because of its strong enforcement powers. The government could detain or cancel government contracts, a serious threat to companies that received large parts of their profits from federal spending. The head of the Labor Department's Wage and Labor Standards Administration estimated that companies covered by the order employed about a third of the workers in the country.

Unfortunately, although the Labor Department's Office of Federal Contract Compliance (OFCC) made some meager efforts to enforce the law for blacks, Mexicans, and other racial or ethnic minorities, it made no effort to do the same for women. In fact, when women's rights leaders met with Labor Secretary James Hodgson in the summer of 1970, he told them he would have to take "a much closer look" at the problem and that he had "no intention of applying literally exactly the same approach to women" as he was doing for minorities.

After NOW provoked protests by congressmen, by its own chapters around the country, and by other women's organizations, Hodgson changed his mind and said the government would require "goals and timetables" for the employment of women, though he added that this would not apply to all jobs since "many occupations sought after by all racial groups have not been sought by women in significant numbers." Women's rights leaders responded that this was outrageous—that women often did not apply for jobs because they knew they would not get them.

NOW also worked to focus public attention and gain public support for the Equal Rights Amendment, a measure that had been introduced into Congress at every session since 1923 and had been defeated the few times it had made its way out of committee. The amendment said: "Equality of rights under the law shall not be denied or abridged by the United States or any state on account of sex." It was designed to erase hundreds of federal and local laws that set separate rules for men and women—laws that restricted married women's property rights and ability to conduct business, that set quotas or barred women from public school and colleges, that set different standards for divorce and family obligations, and that established hour and weight-lifting restrictions used by employers to deny women jobs, promotions, and overtime pay.

Opponents of the amendment—including the AFL-CIO—had long

argued that women were weaker and needed special protection and that the proposal would endanger women's alimony rights and subject them to the draft. Feminists replied that they were being "protected" out of good jobs—and that some of the limitations were absurd—as little as lifting ten pounds in one state, which was less than the weight of an infant child or a bag of groceries.

They also argued that women rarely received alimony, only child support, and that the amendment would not do away with either, but merely award it to the dependent partner in the marriage, whether that happened to be husband or wife. And, they said, if serving in the army was the price of equality, they would be happy to pay. (One feminist quipped that women would probably be sent where their talents could be used best—in Army Intelligence!)

On a local level, the Berkeley Chapter of NOW lobbied for legislation introduced by State Senator Mervyn Dymally which aimed at reversing university discrimination by requiring compensatory hiring, financial aid, free child-care centers, nonsexist textbooks, and women on the California Council for Higher Education.

It also supported fourteen-year-old Vickie Blakeslee's request for a change in the state law that prohibited girls from taking jobs delivering newspapers.

The Princeton, New Jersey, chapter won university financial support for a NOW child-care center. The Long Island chapter obtained American Federation of Teachers support for a proposal to integrate all shop and home economics classes in the Farmingdale school district.

In Chicago, NOW women lobbied successfully for a state constitutional provision to ban sex discrimination. In New York and Pennsylvania, NOW chapters were instrumental in the passage of laws to ban sex discrimination in the sale or rental of housing.

NOW chapters also protested against the bars and restaurants that either excluded women outright or insisted that they be accompanied by men. Women found this humiliating and insulting. Businesswomen and attorneys were unable to attend luncheon meetings with colleagues and clients. Unescorted women were treated as if they were prostitutes.

NOW protests succeeded in ending a men-only "Executive Flight" run by United Airlines between Newark and Chicago. The company had stated, "Executive service was established in response to a desire on the part of businessmen so that they could take off their jackets, loosen their ties, remove their shoes, and relax after a day's work." The company declared that the "men only" restriction "was attached because most men would be hesitant to conduct themselves in this way in mixed company, and also because most women prefer flights with a different atmosphere." It may not have occurred to the airline that there are some "business executives" who happen to be women.

Some critics protested that the whole issue was trivial. (They had said the same thing during sit-ins at Southern lunch counters by black students.) A feminist law student, Jan Goodman, responded that "What is at issue is the indignity and humiliation to a class of people who can be excluded from public places by a male dominated society that can enforce its personal prejudices through law."

# CHAPTER SEVENTEEN THE MOVEMENT SPREADS

At the same time that the National Organization for Women was growing, independent local groups began to organize in various cities under the banner of "Women's Liberation." They were generally young women, some of them political radicals who had been put off by the male chauvinism of the Left, and others were college students or women who had suffered the horror of needing abortions, the frustration of being turned down for the jobs they wanted, and the humiliation of being treated as inferiors by the men who were their friends, their acquaintances, and their colleagues or bosses.

In the beginning, they organized to "rap" about the roots of their oppression. They explored their feelings about their lives as women, and they discovered that many of them had been feeling the same anger and outrage, the same sense of dejection and self-contempt. They realized that their feelings were not "personal" at all, but were the result of a social system that set men over women and denied them the opportunity to fulfill their own needs as human beings.

They took names like the "Women's Liberation Front" and the "Radical Feminists." More and more women came to attend their "consciousness-raising" sessions until they had to split and form new groups so that informal conversation would be possible. They began to publish papers on the topics that concerned them—marriage and housework and women as sex objects.

They held street actions and demonstrations to focus public attention on their demands. One group demanded to speak at a New York State legislative hearing on abortion that had been set up to hear testimony from several men and one nun. In Atlantic City, they threw false eyelashes, padded bras, spiked-heel shoes, and steno pads into a "freedom trash can" set up to receive the symbols of female exploitation represented by the Miss America pageant. (That is where the myth of "bra burning" developed. Actually, feminists have never burned anything.)

Women at the University of North Carolina at Chapel Hill protested against the school's "Bird Watcher's Guide," which printed the photographs of all female students. In Detroit, women draped in black staged a procession past the city morgue "to mourn our dead sisters" who were victims of illegal abortions.

Members of "Bread and Roses" (from the old labor song that commemorates a strike by women textile workers) protested an advertisement run by a Boston radio station that called for "chicks" who could type. They presented the station manager with eight live baby chicks so he could tell the difference between them and women, and they demanded—and got—an hour for a show on women's liberation.

One group held an abortion "speak-out" at which women who had undergone illegal abortions told of the horror and humiliation of the experience. Another picketed the Boston Playboy Club to protest the exploitation of women as sex objects—and a male NOW member joined the line costumed as a bunny! In Los Angeles, women disrupted a CBS stockholders' meeting to protest the insulting view of women on the media—and to demand a weekly program produced by feminists.

These kinds of actions served to educate politicians as well as the general public, partly because the media is much more likely to publicize protest actions (television requires "visual appeal") than to discuss legislative or legal demands. And they forced men and women all over the country to confront the issues and talk about them for the first time.

In New York, feminists set up abortion referral services to help women get around administrative obstacles and high prices that threatened to make abortions as difficult to get as before the passage of the state's liberalized law. Other women set up cooperative day-care centers staffed by men as well as women. Around the country they organized classes to study women's roles in history and their struggle for equality. And they began to publish newspapers and magazines to look at feminist history, to analyze the condition of women, and to report the activities of the new movement.

Groups like the National Association for the Repeal of Abortion Laws (NARAL) and Zero Population Growth were organized to educate the public and provide political and legal leadership in the fight against abortion laws. State chapters lobbied for repeal bills in legislatures. "Reform" bills were introduced in some twenty-nine states, but feminists attacked them because they did not grant all women the right to control their own bodies and instead legalized abortion in the very small minority of cases where women had become pregnant through rape or incest or where there was a threat of deformity to the child.

The effect reached the courts, where proponents of abortion sought to declare the laws unconstitutional and in several cases they succeeded. In the People v. Belous, the California Supreme Court struck down an 1850 abortion law on the grounds that it was vague and violated due process and because it violated a woman's fundamental right to choose whether or not to have children.

In a second case, the People v. Robb, it ruled against a California abortion "reform" law passed in 1967 saying that the law violated the Fourteenth Amendment because it reserved for hospitals the right to determine who was entitled to an abortion, it worked against the poor, and it violated the First Amendment because it permitted a religious belief to influence legislative policy.

Courts in both Washington, D.C., and Wisconsin issued similar rulings, and the cases were appealed to the United States Supreme Court.

Other kinds of organizations began to spring up to answer the special needs of women in every area of life. Federally Employed Women (FEW) was founded in the summer of 1968 by government workers who sought enforcement of an Executive Order issued by President

Johnson that had banned discrimination in federal employment. The president, Daisy Fields, a staff assistant in the personnel division of the Veterans Administration, had been a government worker for twenty-six years. Chapters in other cities continue to be organized.

The Women's Equity Action League (WEAL) was set up as an association of professional women to focus on legal action. One of its first projects was to file complaints charging discrimination in employment by some one hundred colleges and universities that received federal assistance. The woman behind that action was Dr. Bernice Sandler, a professor and educational consultant who taught at the University of Maryland.

Women college professors organized caucuses in their own professional organizations to protest job discrimination and "sexist" teaching and to demand that the groups work for on-campus child-care facilities for faculty, staff, and students. Women in the American Psychological Association, led by Drs. Jo-Ann Evans Gardner and Alice Rossi, charged that modern psychotherapy had perpetuated the myths of male supremacy and contributed to mental illness among women by making them believe it was "masculine" to be assertive and want equality with men.

Caucuses and study groups were also established in the American Political Science Association, the American Sociological Association, and the Modern Language Association. They all protested the fact that recruiters who set up booths at the organizations' meetings and advertised in their journals blatantly discriminated against women by actually specifying "male" for some jobs.

The newsletter published by the Women's Caucus for Political Science mentioned one department chairman who had said, "We don't discriminate against women. We just put all the applications from women at the bottom of the stack; when we run out of qualified men, we consider women."

Women college professors also began to organize and teach courses in women's studies focusing on women's role in the family system, in history, in law, and in literature.

Women journalists organized, and at the 1970 convention of the National Newspaper Guild, they won support for action against sex discrimination, including efforts to end "male only" rules in press clubs and press boxes at sports events. Women at the *Washington Post* persuaded editors to agree to end demeaning references to women. They wouldn't be called "girls" if they were women, the editor said, and they wouldn't be described as "brunettes" or "divorcées" unless the word would likely be used to describe a man in the same situation.

People also became more aware of another part of "the movement" that had existed in the writings of people like Doris Lessing, Marya Mannes, Anais Nin, Brigid Brophy, Mary McCarthy, and Simone de Beauvoir, who filled their novels and essays with incisive comments about the nature of sexism.

Even women tennis players organized, protesting that the prize money paid for their games was only a fraction of that awarded to men. They began by boycotting a match that offered a first prize of $12,500 to men and only $1,500 to women.

In the churches, women protested the male supremacy that has been institutionalized for centuries. The National Association of Women Religious was organized in 1970 at a meeting of some 2,000 nuns in Cleveland, Ohio, to protest their subservience to priests and bishops, and some orders turned into secular groups to avoid that domination.

At the Cleveland meeting, Sister Albertus Magnus McGrath of River Forest, Illinois, protested: "Father says this is a clerical church. I say it's a male church. There is a presumption with regard to women that they're inferior. Under canon law, women are not permitted to testify—nor are children or imbeciles."

Dr. Elizabeth Farians, a Catholic theologian who heads NOW's Task Force on Women and Religion, conducted a protest against the fact that women have been given the right to read the Bible and act as lectors during mass—but only when no men are available, and that women must stand outside the altar rail. She burned the new Missal and sent its ashes, tied with a pink ribbon, to the Bishop of Chicago.

At a "World Congress on the Future of the Church" sponsored by an international theological journal and attended by about eight hundred religious scholars, most of them Catholic, a resolution condemned discrimination against women in the church and called on

Catholics to "examine seriously the possible role of women in the ministry."

Virginia Mills, a member of the United Presbyterian Task Force on Women, told a press conference that "church authorities, usually entirely male, have misused the Bible to reinforce their prejudices against women."

At the American Baptist Convention in 1970, the president of the American Baptist Women expressed "disappointment" that a woman had not been chosen to head that organization and warned that there would be a floor-fight unless a woman was picked the next year. A pamphlet prepared by the Baptist Women stated that they did not have equal opportunities to serve on the church's major boards and committees or to become pastors—and that women pastors received lesser salaries than men.

In 1969, although the National Council of Churches chose its first woman president, Cynthia Wedel, a women's caucus at its 1970 convention accused the Council of having outdated attitudes toward women.

Episcopal women won a victory when their church convention agreed to give them votes in its House of Deputies, a governing body of clergy and laymen. And the Episcopal Diocese of New York approved a change in canon law to allow women to become priests. As the result of a change adopted in 1970, women in the Lutheran Church can be ordained as ministers. Approximately one-quarter of the 235 members of the World Council of Churches allow women ministers, including the Methodists and Presbyterians.

Sandra Eisenberg, at a Hebrew seminary in Philadelphia, sought to storm what may be the oldest bastion of male supremacy in existence by becoming the first female rabbinical student in history.

Many of the women's rights and professional groups joined together at lobbying efforts for legislation. They testified in favor of Representative Edith Green's amendment to extend the Equal Pay Act of 1963 to professional, executive, and technical workers, against the opposition of the Nixon Administration. They supported—and the Nixon Administration opposed—Representative Green's proposal to eliminate the exemption of teachers and other school employees from Title VII, to add "sex" to the section of the Civil Rights Act

(Title VI) that prohibits discrimination in programs receiving federal funds, and to extend the jurisdiction of the United States Civil Rights Commission to the area of sex discrimination.

Organizations like the American Association of University Women, the National Association of Business and Professional Women, the United Auto Workers, and NOW lobbied for the Equal Rights Amendment to the Constitution while sections of organized labor opposed it.

The feminists of the 1970's have encountered the same kind of opposition their predecessors faced a century ago. Critics say they are unsexed women who really want to be men—though that hardly accounts for the demand for the right to abortion. Opponents claim that they are probably ugly old maids who cannot get a husband—though that hardly explains the demand for universal child care. They say that a woman's true vocation is as mother and homemaker—yet they ignore the fact that about 40 percent of all mothers work. They talk about the need for special laws to protect women workers—yet they do not say a word about the kind of protection women need and do not have—the right to maternity leave and protection against being fired for pregnancy or childbirth. They insist that men really have a harder time while women lounge around at home, going to museums and beauty salons in their hours of spare time—yet they are quick to decline any suggestion that they trade places. Virginia Woolf wrote, "Women have served all these centuries as looking-glasses possessing the magic and delicious power of reflecting the figure of man at twice its natural size." Men are not about to forfeit all that without a struggle.

One of the most significant groups in the movement is not really organized at all—it is composed of the thousands of women who have filed complaints of discrimination with human rights agencies at all levels of government. In the first year it was in operation, the Equal Employment Opportunity Commission was shocked to discover that a quarter of its complaints were from women—and the numbers of sex discrimination complaints the EEOC receives every year have increased to 45 percent of the total.

Complaints to the EEOC and other agencies are beginning to pay off. A judge found the Corning Glass Works in Corning, New York, guilty of violating the Equal Pay Act by paying men inspectors more than women. Some three hundred women stand to gain up to $200,000 in back pay.

In another case, a woman working as a wire preparation machine operator at North American Aviation in California discovered when she returned from sick leave that her job had been reclassified "for males only" because of a new order on weight-lifting restrictions for women. When she applied for an inspector's job, she found that that had also been reclassified. The EEOC ruled that her rights had been violated.

Eighteen women who were laid off by Swift & Co., in South Saint Paul, Minnesota, charged that separate seniority lists and job classifications for men and women resulted in their losing their jobs while men with less service stayed on. They sought $170,000 in damages and back pay.

A complaint filed with the New York City Human Rights Commission against the American Broadcasting Company (ABC) declared that women were hired only as secretaries and researchers and were denied the opportunity to work in top jobs as reporters and executives. Over forty women at *Newsweek* magazine also accused management of restricting them to jobs as secretaries and researchers—and after some protests from the editor-in-chief that it was not discrimination but only "a news magazine tradition going back to almost fifty years," agreement was reached to begin promoting women to writing and reporting positions.

A woman pilot who meets all the Federal Aviation Administration regulations for commercial flying filed charges of discrimination against World Airways, Inc. She said that the airline told her she did not fit their "image" of a pilot—"a tall, gray-haired man."

There are no women pilots on major American airlines—in fact, United Airlines openly admits that "pilots must be of the male species," and others set arbitrary physical requirements.

Over forty stewardesses brought a court case against Northwest Airlines on grounds that men who work as pursers do the same jobs they do but get higher salaries. And a union—the Airline Stewards and Stewardesses Association of Chicago sued American, Northeast, and Trans World Airlines because of their policies that women be grounded or fired as soon as it is discovered that they are pregnant.

In 1965, Congresswoman Martha Griffiths of Detroit, Michigan, wrote somewhat sarcastically to the Senior Vice President for Personnel of United Air Lines, "This is in response to your letter of October 4 objecting to married women as stewardesses, a job which apparently requires that a girl serve food and drinks," she said. "You further point out that you are asking a bona fide occupational exception that a stewardess be young, attractive and single. What are you running," she inquired, "an airline or a whorehouse?"

The United States Justice Department had been empowered to bring its own antidiscrimination suits since 1964, but it did not file the first suit on behalf of women until six years later. In 1970, it sought a court order to require Libbey-Owens-Ford, a Toledo, Ohio, glass manufacturer, to hire, train, promote, and pay women equally with men in its five plants. There were only 200 women out of 5,400 workers at the plants. The suit also named the United Glass and Ceramic Workers Union as a defendant and charged that union contracts had set procedures for promotion, layoff, and recall that worked against women.

Another case, which will probably be considered a landmark, was filed by the NAACP Legal Defense Fund, with "friend of the court" briefs by the EEOC, the Justice Department, and NOW. The case, which was appealed to the United States Supreme Court, involved Ida Phillips who had been working fifty-six hours a week as a waitress and earning $2,000 a year plus tips to support her seven children.

Mrs. Phillips applied for a $6,000-a-year, forty-hour-a-week job on an assembly line at the Martin-Marietta plant in Orlando, Florida, and was rejected because she had preschool children. The company admitted that it had no similar policy for *fathers* of preschool children. This was the first sex discrimination case to go to the Supreme Court and the outcome was expected to have a substantial effect on opportunities for the country's millions of working mothers with preschool children.

One of the judges who dissented from the appellate decision commented, "The distinguishing factor seems to be motherhood versus fatherhood. The question then arises: Is this sex-related? To the simple query the answer is just as simple: Nobody—and this includes

Judges, Solomonic or life tenured—has yet seen a male mother. A mother, to oversimplify the simplest biology, must then be a woman." Apparently, his colleagues on the bench did not agree.

In another case, Kathy Kusner, who had ridden in the 1968 Olympics, sued and won her place as the first woman jockey. Women members of the National Maritime Union demanded equal rights to work on freighters as cooks, stewardesses, and galley helpers. The ship owners argued that this would present "a serious potential social and psychological strain on the crew," but the women worried that they would lose pension benefits they had built up by working on the now scarce passenger liners.

As the sentiments and psychology of the "movement" spread, women who never officially joined any organization almost unconsciously began to demand a more equal share of American life. And, as male supremacy is an international system, they were joined by their sisters in other countries throughout the world.

# CHAPTER EIGHTEEN THE STRUGGLE IS INTERNATIONAL

In Australia, women fought for and won a law allowing married women to hold civil service jobs. Until then, women working for the government had to leave their jobs when they married, and married women were not hired—except on a temporary basis as they were needed.

In New Delhi, India, Punjabi women demonstrated against a proposed law that would bar women from inheriting property—a right they received only recently. One of the arguments made by advocates of the bill was that women's property rights have caused bad relations between brothers and sisters. (No mention was made of what the previous system did to relations between brothers.)

In France, feminists are working for day-care centers, the right to abortion, executive jobs for women, and greater representation in Parliament and the government. As a result of feminist action, laws were passed just recently to give married women equal rights in determining where their families will live and in writing bank checks without their husband's approval.

All over the world, the movement for women's rights has become a vital, growing force making demands on society for a reversal of traditional laws and patterns that have kept women in servitude. And the demands are the same in every country—equality in jobs and education, day care, access to abortion and contraception, full legal rights, and representation in government.

In Canada, women in Quebec organized a demonstration at the time of the American August 26 protests to demand equality in jobs and education, free child care, and free abortions on demand. Members of the women's federation of Quebec's Liberal Party called for the abolition of the separate women's division, the full participation of women in the activities of the party, and more representation in the National Assembly.

The first mass meeting of England's women's liberation movement was held in March, 1970, when about 500 women met at Oxford University and made demands similar to those of their Canadian sisters. In England, women comprise 35 percent of the labor force—about 9 million out of over 25 million workers. Their wages are as low as 65 percent of men's salaries for the same jobs. More than 50 percent of women workers earn under twenty-four dollars a week, and only one in thirty earns the average men's wage. About 56 percent of English women workers are married.

The demand for equal pay for women was raised by the British suffragists in the 1800's but it took until 1970 for Parliament to pass an equal pay act—and that was not scheduled to take effect until 1975.

In London, in the summer of 1970, thirty women journalists stormed the barriers of "El Vino," a famous Fleet Street pub that caters to reporters. Women are not permitted to stand at the bar.

Bills have been introduced into Parliament to ban discrimination against women in public facilities like bars and restaurants and to give women a fairer share of the family's property in divorce. Today, British women have no rights to property acquired during a marriage. And unless women go to court, they have no influence over their children's religious training, which is legally in the father's hands.

Women are less than 25 percent of the students in higher education. They are not allowed membership on the London Stock Exchange, and women workers are handicapped by restrictions on overtime and night work. Queen Elizabeth seems to be on the side of the feminists; she has stated that "it is becoming more generally recognized that the home is not the only place for women."

In France, the law passed in 1969 also gives wives an almost equal say with husbands about how they bring up their children. The new law said decisions had to be made jointly—except that if there was disagreement, the husband's opinion had to be accepted and the wife could only challenge it in court. In France, where women total 33 percent of the work force, they did not win the right to vote until 1946, and they could not have their own bank accounts until 1965. It is only recently that women could legally receive mail without their husband's interference. The French fashion magazine *Elle* has sponsored women's liberation conferences around the country.

In Italy, where some young women still must drag chaperones along on dates, women's liberation groups have sprung up in half a dozen large cities. One of their major demands is for abortion. Years of struggle resulted in the legalization of divorce in 1970. Italian husbands have complete control over family decisions—and they can even write them into their wills and perpetuate them after death! A woman with children cannot get a passport without her husband's permission, and until 1968, women faced up to two years in jail for adultery while men who were unfaithful to their wives were punished only if they publicly kept a woman in their own home or elsewhere.

Women make up about 25 percent of the work force (about 27 percent of Italian women work), but the numbers have decreased in the last ten years as the result of discrimination that condemns them to the lowest-paid jobs. Over 50 percent of the women seeking work do not have even high school educations. Moreover, efforts to provide child-care facilities have proved inadequate, and there is still an attitude that "a woman's place is in the home." Discussion groups and rallies have been held to focus on feminist demands and to build the women's movement in Italy.

In Germany, in 1969, Edith Neumann, a Social Democrat and a member of that party's executive committee of the city of Kiel, protested the condescending attitude of the party toward women and was told it was women's own fault if they did not get more opportunities. The last straw was the party's national election slogan: "We have the right men."

When protests failed, she placed an advertisement in a local newspaper charging that the Social Democrats had renounced the support of women by their actions and she urged women to vote for their opponents. She was expelled from her party post immediately by an all-male party tribunal—but she had made her point in the press.

Women's liberation groups have been organized in Berlin and West Germany, and cooperative day-care centers have been set up in abandoned stores in Berlin, Munich, Hamburg, and Cologne. In Frankfurt, demonstrations and petitions demanded the repeal of restrictive abortion laws. Women also protested the fact that they get paid less than men for the same work and that although they comprise 33 percent of the work force, only 3 percent of the country's top jobs are held by women.

Dutch women have organized into the "Dolle Minas" (Mad Minas) named for nineteenth-century feminist Wilhelmina (Mina) Drucker who fought for women's right to vote—and was consequently described as "mad." The Dolle Minas seek equality in jobs and pay, free abortions, and the end of the system that defines work as a male responsibility and housekeeping as women's work.

They have also protested against the men who degrade them with remarks and wolf whistles by showing how it feels to have the shoe on the other foot. They attracted worldwide attention by staging a demonstration in which women whistled and made caustic comments at passing men. And they attached pink ribbons to the doors of men's public toilets to protest the fact that there are no such facilities for women.

In Denmark, women, who are 33 percent of the country's workers, have protested the unequal pay they receive. One group made its point by going on buses and paying only 80 percent of the fare. The Danish social insurance system classifies married women as "nonsupporters" and pays them lower unemployment and sick benefits than men.

In Norway, nearly a century after the publication of Henrik Ibsen's "A Doll's House," women are seeking equal pay, and they are demanding that school doctors be made to teach girls fourteen and over how to use birth control methods. In Ibsen's influential play, written in 1879, the husband, Helmer, tells his wife: "Before all else you are a wife and a mother," and Nora responds: "That I no longer believe. I think that before all else I am a human being, just as much as you are—or, at least, I will try to become one."

The loss of over 15 million men in World War II has ironically given Russian women the opportunity to do jobs that require great physical labor while still restricting the top jobs to men. Nevertheless, Russian women have substantial equality and they earn equal pay for the same work. Women drive tractors and street cars, lay cables, and are employed in the construction trades. They are radio announcers, and three out of four of the country's doctors. Nearly 80 percent of women work at least part time, and women are nearly 50 percent of the labor force.

Still, the more skilled jobs in the blue collar trades, the professions, and administration are held by men. While a lady is out operating a crane, a man is likely to be looking over a project's blueprints. Russian women are no longer bound by the czarist rules that required them to obey their husbands in everything. One woman wrote: "Why should I consider my husband the head of the family? We earn about the same, but when you figure out how much he spends on drinking, then my family lives to a great extent on my income!"

A 1967 report to the United Nations Commission on Human Rights said there are over two million slaves in the world—most are Arab, African, or Asian women. Iraq allows legal bigamy, and concubinage still exists in Turkey. Nevertheless, even women in those repressive countries are demanding their rights.

The Tanzania Women's Association asked the government to give women the right to more than one husband as long as men have a right to more than one wife. The government announced that the women were "too emotional" and one man expressed the popular sentiment in a letter to the editor of a major newspaper which said that "no sane man would enter a contract to share a woman with another man when he could have a whole wife or two to himself." In Muslim countries, there are signs on mosques that say: "Women and dogs and other impure objects are not permitted to enter."

In Indonesia, women have held demonstrations in an effort to win the legal right to prevent their own husbands from taking second wives. In 1967, South Korean women's organizations campaigned against the existence of geisha-like "kisaeng houses" for men.

And even within the United Nations, the battle goes on. The United Nations Commission on the Status of Women met in Geneva in 1970 and passed a resolution urging United Nations Secretary-General U Thant to hire more women at top level United Nations jobs. Esmeralda Arboleda de Cuevas Cancino of Colombia said that the director of the United Nations Division on Human Rights had asked her husband, the Mexican representative to the United Nations, to try to make her withdraw the motion. He replied that he did not interfere with his wife's official actions.

In some countries, women still do not have the right to vote or hold office, and in others their rights are limited. Swiss women may vote in local elections in only 9 out of 23 cantons and have no federal voting rights at all.

Women in Portugal may vote and run for office but they must fulfill educational requirements not set for men. Thirteen other nations have similar restrictions—nine of them are Arab countries where women have historically occupied a subservient position. They include Saudi Arabia, Jordan, Iraq, Yemen, Kuwait, Libya, and Afghanistan, where women have no political rights at all; the Syrian Arab Republic, where they may vote if they meet special educational requirements; and the Sudan, where they may run for office but cannot vote. Women also lack political equality in Guatemala (they, but not men, must be literate to vote), in Nigeria, the Congo, and in the small European states of San Marino and Liechtenstein.

Women do vote and hold office in some 114 countries, but they serve in the parliaments of only 55 and they do not actually share political power in any of them.

In the United States in 1970, women held 13 out of 535 seats in Congress. A 1963 study by the United States Women's Bureau found that both here and abroad there was only token representation of women in national legislatures and in the top policy-making positions in government. Canada had 11 women out of a national legislature of 367. In England, there were 24 women among the 630 members of the House of Commons. Thirteen women out of 859 served in the French Senate and National Assembly. In Greece, 3 women were among 300 delegates in the Chamber of Deputies. And in Italy, 28 women served out of 845.

The story was not very different in Communist countries. Only 25 women held seats out of 1,378 in the Soviet Council of Union and the Council of Nationalities, and there were 2 out of 33 on the Soviet Presidium. Four women were among the 587 members of Yugoslavia's Federal People's Assembly, and China had only 290 women out of 4,060 who held national legislative office. The story in Latin America was the same. There was 1 woman out of 326 members of Brazil's Chamber of Deputies, 6 women out of 232 in the legislature of Colombia, and 6 out of 236 in the legislature of Mexico.

The only female heads of state in the world who wield any real power are on the Asian continent. Sirimavo Bandaranaike of Ceylon became the world's first woman premier in 1960 (serving until 1965), Indira Gandhi was made prime minister of India in 1966, and Golda Meir was chosen premier of Israel in 1969. Nevertheless, even in those countries, the Women's Bureau survey found only 4 women out of the 187 Senators and representatives of Ceylon, 52 women among the 745 legislators of India, and 1 woman out of 120 in the Knesset of Israel.

In Africa, women were similarly excluded. Ten women served out of 104 in the National Assembly of Ghana—and they were in seats reserved for women. One woman out of 74 was a member of the House of Representatives of Sierra Leone. Five women out of 214 were part of the legislature of South Africa—which bans blacks totally from political participation. (One of the women members, Helen Suzman, has been the most prominent legislator to speak out against apartheid.)

In many countries around the world, women are limited not only to token representation in political office, but they are also refused an equal opportunity to work for their own governments. Until 1945, French women were kept out of the diplomatic service and were denied the right to serve as judges in overseas possessions. In Italy, it took a legislative decree of 1963 to declare that women could be elected or appointed to all public offices. Until 1958, women who were teachers or who worked for the Dutch government could be fired when they married. Swiss women still may be fired from government jobs when they marry. Ironically, in two of the countries where women have been heads of state, women face legal discrimination in government jobs. Women in Ceylon may not join the civil service, and married women in India cannot hold jobs in the foreign or administrative service, which includes the senior officials of the government. Women in these positions may be asked to resign when they marry. The same rule holds for women who work for the government of Sierra Leone.

In New Zealand, thousands of women government workers have been paid less than men for the same jobs. In 1960, the government approved a three-year program to end those inequities. And even in countries where there are no official barriers, women are restricted to the least rewarding jobs. In Canada, only 2 percent of the women who work for the government have administrative or professional posts.

The record for legal abortions around the world is mixed, but whether they go to trained physicians or medical quacks, women continue to refuse to bear unwanted children. There are 30 million abortions performed in the world every year, compared to 115 million live births, a ratio of one to four.

England provides abortion as part of the National Health Service though if there is no physical reason to terminate pregnancy it requires psychiatric examinations to prove that the pregnancy would endanger a woman's mental health. Women are still forced to undergo compulsory pregnancy unless they can convince psychiatrists (usually male) that having a baby would drive them crazy!

In Italy, abortions are against the law, but they are common and easy to get. There is one abortion for every live birth, four times the rate in the United States.

In Bulgaria, Hungary, Japan, Poland, Czechoslovakia, and Yugoslavia, abortions are cheap, safe, and legal. In Sweden, Denmark, and Norway, women need hospital and psychiatric approval.

Abortion is illegal in Puerto Rico and Mexico, but it is performed openly in clinics. In fact, women in all kinds of societies have frequently found some way to get around male prohibitions of abortion. In the Rif tribes of North Africa, men could divorce or kill their wives for having abortions. However, both contraceptives and abortions were available in the "women's market" which men could not enter.

The one country of the world that is looked upon as a model by feminists is Sweden, where women still do not have full equality, but where the government has set as its goal the elimination of the sex-role system. In a speech to the Women's National Democratic Club in Washington, D.C., in June, 1970, Swedish Prime Minister Olof Palme declared: "Nobody should be forced into a predetermined role on account of sex" and he said that in Sweden, "If a politician today should declare that the woman ought to have a different role than the man and that it is natural that she devotes more time to the children, he would be regarded to be of the Stone Age."

Sweden has had a history of feminist protest similar to that in the United States. An eighteenth-century writer and poet, Hedvig Charlotta Nordenflycht, had called for the admission of women to the professions, declaring that women's faults were not inherent, but the result of their perverted education. In 1856, the pioneer of Swedish feminism, Fredrika Bremer, published a novel called *Hertha* which explored the difficulties faced by unmarried women.

The modern feminist debate began in Sweden in the late 1950's. Women had already won almost all their legal rights. The first women's organizations had been founded at the end of the nineteenth century. Married women were given control of their own property. Women were admitted to the universities in 1870. In 1921 the Marriage Act changed the law that had made husbands the guardians of their wives, and that same year women voted for the first time. In 1939, a law declared that women could not be fired for engagement, marriage, pregnancy, or childbirth.

The new Swedish feminism began with an essay by Eva Moberg, "The Conditional Release of Women," that protested the fact that women alone were forced to play two roles. They could work alongside men for pay, but they also had to do their traditional work at home. She declared that both women and men should work outside the home and share the tasks of housework and caring for children. She called for the abolition of marriage as a career and for all women to become economically independent.

The essay aroused a storm of debate. In a letter addressed to "Mrs. Housewife," Eva Moberg asserted that "the entire housewife system must be dismantled." She explained that she did not say this to denigrate housewives but because, "As long as it is taken for granted that it is she who is chiefly responsible for home and children, just so long will she go on being handicapped professionally, and the gainful professions and occupations, as hitherto, will remain chiefly a male prerogative."

As long as many women choose to stay home as housewives, other women would have a double-life role forced on them, she states. Why? "Because just so long will housework and looking after children be regarded as a woman's—and only a woman's—business. And as long as housework is a woman's business, just so long will society's reluctance to provide service facilities, e.g., day nurseries, continue; just so long will employers hesitate to invest in women, women in practice will remain a reserve labor force, "women's work" will be worse paid than men's, and men—in spite of all the fine words spoken round dinner tables—will continue to underrate housework."

She pointed out that, "The male labor market has always been based on one self-evident condition: that somebody else is doing all the little practical jobs which need to be done for an employee and his children—cooking, washing, tidying up and mending. As for the female labor market, it has also been founded on an equally self-evident axiom: that a woman employee has another, more important job on the side."

Eva Moberg called for a change in "the housewife system," declaring that society must pay for child care by providing day-care centers and giving parents financial aid, that most housework should be done by paid workers, and that "every healthy adult male should wait on himself."

As the people of Sweden talked about the ideas she had raised, they came to the conclusion, said Prime Minister Palme, that "the role of woman could not be changed if that of the man was not also changed." And they realized that these roles were established very early in life.

"In Sweden it is usual that parents give mechanical toys to boys and dolls to girls," explained Palme, and he said that this led to a situation where few girls chose technical fields and few boys went into nursing. Now both boys and girls are required to study sewing, cooking, and child care as well as wood and metal crafts in an effort to break the established cultural patterns.

Palme called his speech "The Emancipation of Man," asserting that men would gain by the abolition of the "sex-role system." He pointed out that men shouldered the economic burden of supporting their families, they were under great pressure to be aggressive and not show their feelings, and they had higher suicide rates and died earlier than women. "The greatest disadvantage with the male sex-role," he said, "is that the man has too small a share in the upbringing of the children." He suggested reduced working hours for *both* parents of small children so that they could share the responsibilities and rewards of caring for them. And having fathers at home would counteract the false picture of masculinity presented by television, comics, and the movies where only men are "tough and hard-boiled wildwest heroes, agents, supermen, and soldiers," said Palme.

These same recommendations were made in a report by the Swedish government to the United Nations in 1968. It said that "No rapid advancement of women in employment and the professions, politics, trade union activity, etc., is possible as long as men fail to assume that share of the work of the home which falls to them as husbands and fathers. The expression 'male emancipation' has, therefore, been coined in Sweden to denote the right of a husband to remain at home while the children are small where it is found more appropriate for the mother to devote herself to gainful employment."

The report to the United Nations called for an end to the idea that husbands are responsible for supporting their wives, because it was "a direct obstacle to the economic independence of women and their ability to compete on equal terms in the labor market." It called for a shared responsibility between husbands and wives, explaining that "the individual employer considered the risk of women's leaving his service on marriage too high to justify the investment of training and promoting them. The character of matrimony as an institution for the support of woman according to the occidental tradition has thus come to be an indirect obstacle to her emancipation in modern industrial society," said the report.

Women in Sweden have not yet achieved equality—they earn only 75 percent of what men earn (compared to 58 percent for the United States)—in spite of the fact that from 1960 through 1965, special lower pay scales for women that had been established by union contracts were abolished. They are concentrated in low-paying fields as saleswomen, office workers, and nurses. They rarely have jobs that can lead to the higher levels of private industry and they continue to be almost invisible in the top levels of government. In 1966, 80 percent of full-time men workers earned over $3,600 while 70 percent of women received less than that. In spite of the notion that men and women should share housework and child care, nearly 690,000 (over 57 percent) of women not working in 1966 said it was because of their home duties compared to 6,800 (under 2 percent) of the men. Only 42 percent of Swedish women work, compared to 84 percent of men.

The government is seeking to encourage men to share the responsibility of child care. All workers, men and women, can take off fifteen days a year to look after children or take care of other domestic matters. Some of the cities have begun to provide "samaritans" who look after children at home when they are ill. Part-time work has proved successful. Companies perked up their interest when they discovered that the average productivity of two women who worked part time was higher than that of one man who worked full time.

The government's ultimate goals are salaries and fringe benefits for men or women who stay home to look after children on the same basis as they are given to workers in traditional jobs.

In Sweden the law banning contraception was repealed in 1938 and abortion is allowed if a woman's life or physical and mental health is threatened by a birth, if the pregnancy is the result of rape, or if it is thought that the child will be born deformed or diseased—not a very liberal statute from a feminist point of view. In 1965, some 6,000 legal abortions were performed compared to 123,000 live births.

Today, women in Sweden have begun to break down the age-old prejudices. Women operate cranes on construction sites (there are more women in these jobs than men), they work in mines, and Turi Wideroe, who works for the Scandinavian Airlines System, is the first woman pilot for a major airline in the Western world.

Yet, "male chauvinism" still exists. A woman who wanted to compete in an all-male cross-country ski race in 1969 disguised herself with a beard and crossed the finish line ahead of many of the male entries. She was discovered later when one man saw her beard bob up and down and jerked it off. In 1970, the organizers of the race ordered a close check of contestants' beards.

# CHAPTER NINETEEN THE MESSAGE OF ANTHROPOLOGY

It is "natural" for parents to love and take care of their children—except that in ancient Greece, Rome, and China, and in the early centuries of Western European civilization, infants were often put out in the road to die of starvation or the elements or to be picked up by strangers and raised as slaves or servants.

It is "natural" for men to be the providers and do the heavy work in society—except that there are about four times as many societies where women carry the burdens, and numerous places where women work to put food on the table while their husbands sit around and gossip.

It is "natural" for women to do the cooking and housework for their families—except that there are societies where the men also tend to these tasks.

You have probably never heard of most of these societies—they exist today or in the past in places like Micronesia, Africa, and Asia. Yet, they are important to us because they prove that many of the stereotypes of male and female roles are not "natural" at all in the biological sense. They do not result from the demands of biology as much as from the demands of culture. And as the conditions of our culture change, so can those sex roles. A look at some of the strange differences in sex roles in foreign cultures and at the changes that have evolved even in our own culture over the past few thousand years is both fascinating and instructive.

Anthropologists do not know of any societies that have not been male controlled. Power has always been centered in the men. Most societies are also "patrilineal"—inheritance and descent is traced through the father—and "patrilocal"—a man brings his new wife to live with or near his parents.

Societies also are divided according to their forms of marriage. Monogamy, where one man has one wife, is the rule only in a few societies. The most common practice is polygyny, where men who can afford it have more than one wife. In systems with concubinage, the women taken after the first wife do not have equal status—they are more like servants. There is also polyandry, where one woman has several husbands, and group marriage, where several men and women are communally married—both of which are very rare.

This all goes to show that it is not "natural" for marriages to be made up of one man and one woman—it is a cultural development that seems to answer our needs best and to fit most easily into our value system.

Some societies reject the "woman's role" that Western civilization has established, with work, child care, and housekeeping organized in a totally different fashion. Others make women into such menial drudges that American society would be hailed as the symbol of total emancipation.

Anthropologist Margaret Mead has studied several island cultures. Many of her studies were made in New Guinea. There, the women of the Mundugumor tribe are as active, independent and aggressive as men. They dislike having and taking care of children and avoid it where possible. Boys and girls grow up with very similar personalities. Women do most of the work, yet it is a patriarchal society—men are in control.

Among the Tchambuli, also in New Guinea, women fish and sell their catch in the market while their husbands, who wear jewelry and love to dance and paint, do the family shopping.

The Alorese of Eastern Indonesia consider physical work beneath the dignity of men. The men sit and chat while women and young people do heavy labor. Even in childhood, girls start to work earlier than boys, and their work is harder. Both boys and girls help to care for younger children while their mothers are working.

Some 50,000 Otomi Indians live in one section of Mexico maintaining the customs of their ancestors who inhabited this region before the Spanish conquest of the 1500's. It would not be unusual to see an Otomi man riding on a donkey while his wife plods behind, with a load of corn and pots and pans hanging from a wooden yoke that bends her shoulders.

Women plant corn and harvest it, care for their children, and cook for their families while their husbands lie in the shade and drink pulque, a kind of liquor made from cactus plants.

In Samoan society, work is based on age and status, not on sex. Samoan children wander easily from one set of relations to another. They are not dependent for security only on their parents, and their affections—and aggressions—are directed toward many adults, not just two.

The roles of men and women in the Manu and Arapesh cultures are also very similar. Both men and women participate in Manu economic and religious affairs. And among the Arapesh, both men and women share the role of caring for newborn children. In fact, after the birth of his baby, an Arapesh father stays home from work—a kind of "paternity leave."

In some societies, men work—but their obligations are to their sisters, not their wives. The Trobriand Islanders are a matrilineal society—a man traces his descent not through his father, but through his maternal uncle, and it is his task to provide food for his sister. His wife is given food by her brother.

Until the British occupation in the nineteenth century, the Nayar of India had similar customs, with a twist. Husbands did not live with wives; they "visited" them at night. Women could have several "visiting husbands," and when there were children, the fathers announced their parenthood, but they did not support their families or have any rights over their children. The women lived with their brothers, sisters, mother, and maternal aunts and uncles. The brothers and uncles supported the household—and at night they went "visiting" elsewhere.

Italian journalist Oriana Fallaci wrote about one matrilineal society, the Negri Sembilan people of Malaya, where land is handed down to daughters. The women propose to the men, support them, and make decisions for the family. She talked to one woman who had sent her husband home to his mother. "He didn't want to work," she explained, "so I threw him out. It's time that men too learned how to manage a bit themselves."

However, the women of this society are not its political rulers. They can vote but cannot hold office. And they are still responsible for the care of their children. Though the husband is not considered the head of his family's household, neither is the wife: that position is held by her elder brother.

In most societies, the family is an economic unit. In fact, it is probably more accurate to describe it that way than to say that it is a man and woman and their children. For example, among the Todas of India, female infanticide reduces the number of women available to marry. When a woman marries a man, she becomes the wife of all his brothers as well. No one is very concerned about who is the real father of each of her children.

Sometimes some of the brothers have their own wives. This custom has been increasing as female infanticide decreases. When this occurs it becomes a group marriage. If the brothers live in different villages, the woman spends a month at a time with each of them. Jealousy is considered bad manners. Though it might seem that women are in charge in Toda society, in fact it is patriarchal, patrilineal, and patrilocal. And nobody thinks it strange that Toda husbands do most of the cooking!

The Marquesas Islanders in the South Pacific live in a society where there are two or three men to every woman. There, a man marries a woman and, in order to build up his wealth by adding to his work force, he welcomes "subsidiary husbands" to the house. If he is wealthy, he might even find one or two wives and make it a group marriage, but there will always be more men than women in the arrangement.

Group marriage existed in the early times of Western civilization as well. In his reports on the Gallic Wars, Julius Caesar wrote about a society in ancient Britain where "ten and twelve have wives common among them, especially brothers and brothers and parents with children. If any children are born they are considered as belonging to those men to whom the maid was first married."

However, it has been rare in the history of civilization that women have had more than one husband. In most cases, it has worked the other way around—and even today polygyny exists in some of the so-called civilized countries of the world—especially in the Middle East.

At the end of the nineteenth century, for example, one million Bagandas lived in Uganda, Central Africa. Because of male infanticide and losses in war, there were three times as many women as men—and they were considered an important economic resource. Wives were the providers in this society. While men worked a few hours in the morning and afternoon, the women labored in the fields from dawn to dusk. The wife's most important role was having children—most had about ten—and their children did not live with their own parents, but with their father's brothers.

Angie Brooks of Liberia who became the second woman President of the United Nations General Assembly in 1969 (the first was Vijaya Lakshmi Pandit of India in 1953), tells a story of the bitter oppression of women in the British Cameroons in 1947. The story had come to the attention of the United Nations Trusteeship Council.

*A girl was grinding corn in the small space in front of her father's hut. She was about thirteen years old, a fine child clad in her homespun dress. Two or three men walked down the road, looking from side to side; they stopped, looked hard at the girl who, quite unconscious of their looks, continued her back-breaking task.*

*Then the leader or "Chinda" as he was called, stepped forward, dragged the child to her feet, marked her forehead with a piece of red camwood and stripped off her clothes. The girl howled like a wounded animal—she was doomed. Her father came out and knew the mark meant she was branded.*

*Off the "Chinda" and his men went; their day's work for the King had been done. (The king was the eighty-year-old "Fon of Bikum.")*

*Next day, Papa, arrayed in his tribal splendor, set off for the*

> *King's Compound. The girl, with nothing but a string of large beads around her neck, came sobbing behind. They came to the King's Compound; guards stood in costume with erect spears. The King sat on the throne, a leopard under his feet. About 100 of his 600 wives stood around him in a semi-circle—naked—as was the privilege and custom of the "King's Own."*
>
> *The father stepped forward, bent his knees so that, although bent forward, he was still on his feet, clapped his hands three times, then standing upright dragged his daughter forward, threw her on the ground in front of the King, who stepped forward and put his right foot on top of the girl's body, which meant, "I accept this piece of cargo."*

Angie Brooks said that the Fon's wives told United Nations investigators that they were "living with the Fon according to the natural law and custom."

Polygyny has been common in Western society too—at least in its beginnings. The ancient Hebrews were a strongly patriarchal people who practiced polygyny, concubinage and slavery, though it was more likely to occur among the rich than among commoners. As in most nonliterate cultures, women were thought of as property and were bought with money or service. Jacob spent twenty years working for Laban to buy his daughters Leah and Rachel. Among the Hebrews, a man could either sell his daughters or they could be taken by men for payment of debts.

In another part of the world, the Chinese were practicing a form of male dominance so oppressive that Chinese women had one of the highest suicide rates in the world. It was a system that lasted for over two thousand years, until the beginning of this century.

The Chinese practiced monogamy, but those who could afford it took concubines. That practice was outlawed when the Communist Chinese came to power, but it was legal in the British protectorate of Hong Kong until 1969, and it continues illegally today. Women were considered so useless and inferior that infant girls could be killed at will. Girls stayed at home while their brothers went to school, and when they were older, they stayed within the family compound while the men went out on business or to visit gambling parlors, opium dens, and houses of prostitution.

Women were prevented from straying by the custom of footbinding that made it physically painful for them to walk very far on their own. One old woman told Oriana Fallaci about this custom. "Feet could not be more than three and one-half inches long. You began to bind them when you were five years old, using strips of cotton three-quarters of an inch wide and two yards long. You began young because at that age the bones are still soft. You bound all your toes except the big toe, and each day you bound them tighter until the bones broke and the toes would bend easily under the soles of your foot. You had to stay in bed until the bones had set, and you had great pain."

Small feet were supposed to be beautiful, said the woman. "My mother used to say that girls with big feet did not get a husband, and that only peasants and servants had big feet. In fact, an upper-class man who wanted to marry an upper-class woman would ask, 'How short are your feet?' If they were not short enough, he could cancel the marriage contract."

She recalled, "In my day, there was nothing more shameful than being born a woman. When a girl was born, her family would go into mourning, and the girl quickly had to learn obedience to her father and her brothers. When she married, a girl had to learn obedience to her husband and her mother-in-law. And she did not meet her husband at all until the marriage ceremony itself. Often the husband was much younger than she was. My sister was eighteen when she married a husband seven years old. She was a mother to him while she waited for him to be old enough to make her pregnant, but the boy died when he was twelve and so my sister became a widow without even being a real wife or a real mother.

"Naturally, widows could not remarry, and many parents asked them to starve themselves to death so that they would not be a drag on the family. Some starved themselves to death, because once they were dead they would at last count for something, and the family would spend a lot of money on a fine funeral and put up an arch in the garden with the inscription, 'To the faithful wife.' "

Things were not very different on the other side of the East China Sea. The Japanese practiced female infanticide, and those that lived were ordered about by their fathers before marriage and their husbands afterward. In fact, if women were widowed, they had to bow to the orders of their sons. In parts of old Japan, a four-year-old boy could order his mother around as well as the other women of the house.

Women were barred from any public or political activity along with children and mental defectives.

The Muslim culture was equally oppressive to women. Even today, untold numbers of women still live in *purdah*—confined to their homes—and others who are allowed to go out are forced to cover their faces with veils and their bodies with cloaks.

Muslim men can have several wives. Some take concubines, and it was once common for young girls to be kidnapped or sold into bondage as servants, prostitutes, or concubines—it was called "white slavery," and it still exists in some Arab countries today.

Arab women—sometimes children—still marry men they have never seen. They must go to court to get a divorce, but their husbands only have to say "talak, talak, talak" and they are repudiated—with no alimony required. However, change is beginning as some Muslim women become educated and demand the end of their secondary status and as some government leaders westernize their countries.

At the same time that European, African, and Asian cultures were degrading and exploiting women, in the United States there were societies founded on very different ideas. They were tribes of American Indians such as the Hopi and the Crow and the Navaho. They gave women a status they did not have elsewhere. Among the Hopis of the Arizona desert, for example, women are almost dominant. The family is *matrilineal* and *matrilocal*—often a woman and her husband, their daughter and her husband, and their granddaughter all live together. Boys inherit tribal offices from their mother's brothers. And when there is a divorce, she doesn't go home to mother—he does!

Our society today is *patriarchal*—the man is considered the "head of the household" even on government census forms, but feminists are working to bring about a new system that is neither matriarchal nor patriarchal but is rather a sharing of power and responsibility.

This brief look at other cultures should make it clear that there is no one "natural" way of living together. If you want to say that something is "proper" because it has existed in many societies for many years, you would have to condone polygyny, female concubines, forced marriages between young girls and old men or between youths who have never met, infanticide, and the treatment of women as slaves and servants. We may regard these practices as brutal and cruel, but they have all been accepted by diverse societies for thousands of years. Some exist even today.

Anthropology, however, has some important lessons for us. Margaret Mead points out that the Arapesh are a peaceful people. "Cultures like the Arapesh show how easily, where parents do not discriminate strongly between the sexes of their children and men take over a nurturing role, this [aggressive] drive in males may be muted."

Aggression can be seen in street gangs that engage in minor crime or just bully other children. The boys gather together to prove that they are not "sissies"—which means that they are not like girls.

An emphasis on violence and aggression can have other negative consequences. The demand for bravery was so strong in the society of the American Plains Indians that some men who could not meet those standards gave up and dressed themselves as women.

Obviously, just because something has always been done in a particular society does not mean that it is the best way for things to continue. Anthropologists say that the division of labor between men and women seems to have little to do with biological abilities or limitations. In some societies, women stay indoors because they are considered very delicate; in others, they carry the heavy burdens because their heads are supposed to be stronger. Margaret Mead points out that in some cultures, women fish while men make speeches; in still others men drive oxen while women make religious offerings.

A Navaho Indian refused to be photographed milking a goat because "It wouldn't look right"—it was considered women's work. Yet, Navaho men find nothing wrong with cooking or caring for children. But whatever *men* do in different cultures, *that* is the activity that is considered important, and in many societies, men are not sure of their masculinity unless they can prevent women from doing some activity that is assigned exclusively to them.

The household work—cooking, cleaning, and caring for children—has nearly always been done by women, and the hunting, herding large animals, metal and stone crafts, and boat building are almost always men's work. Of course, most men no longer hunt, herd animals, or do the other tasks performed by their early ancestors. Food gathering, manufacturing, and construction have been revolutionized by technology, and both men and women are involved in them. Why, then, since housework has been similarly revolutionized (we no longer bake our own bread or tutor our own children), can't men share in those tasks?

Today, people are seeking to find new forms of social living that will be more humane and satisfying for everyone. One reflection of this search is a current interest in communal living. The most interesting experiment along those lines is underway now in Israel, where about 80,000 people live in agricultural kibbutz communities. In those societies, families are no longer economic units, and mothers no longer are responsible for the care of their children.

The kibbutz was organized by people who had grown up in the Jewish communities of Eastern Europe where patriarchy reigned supreme and women's only role was to care for their husbands and children. The Israelis were determined to create a society where women would be equal with men, and they believed that this could not be done as long as women were forced to continue in their traditional roles.

When a man and woman on a kibbutz marry, the man does not become the "head of the household" as in the traditional Jewish family. In fact, the woman may keep her own name. Sometimes couples do not have a legal marriage ceremony until their first child is due. And they both continue to hold their jobs. If they have a child, the new baby is taken to the infants' house usually four days after its birth. The mother may visit to nurse the baby, but the child is cared for by trained people who are also responsible for several other infants.

Between the ages of one and two, the child moves to the toddlers' house; at three and one-half to four it goes to a kindergarten house; at about seven to a children's house and at thirteen to the youth house. The children are cared for by professional attendants and taught by teachers while they live and play and eat together with boys and girls of their own age. Parents visit the babies in the evening, and when children are old enough, they come to their parents' room for a few hours each night. The children are given a great deal of responsibility over their own lives, making joint decisions about their social and cultural activities, and setting their own rules about behavior and discipline.

It had been thought that it was necessary for children to be raised by their mothers—or at least by one woman. However, some American psychologists who have studied the kibbutz discovered that the children were actually healthier than children raised in American society. They came to the conclusion that infants and children need care and security, but that this does not have to be provided by one person only.

The children on a kibbutz did not become emotionally involved with only one or two people. Since food, shelter, and security were provided by the community at large, they were less afraid of losing the love and protection of their parents. Instead, they had strong ties to others of their age group and to the community as a whole. They were better adjusted than American children and showed little emotional disturbance. There was no drug addiction or juvenile delinquency problem. There were no parents who beat their children or mistreated them or sought to exercise authoritarian power over them.

Yet, at the same time that women of the kibbutz have rejected the idea that their main purpose in life is to bear and raise children, they are still not totally equal. Women are often required to do the "women's" jobs that have less prestige—jobs in the kitchen, the laundry, and the nurseries—while men are more likely to be high school teachers, drive tractors, or administer the business affairs of the farm.

Nevertheless, the Israelis teach us that men and women can be happy living by rules that totally contradict everything we have always been taught was "natural." Rather than accept the past and consider it "fate" that women are limited by their roles of wife and mother, they have begun to consider the notion that there should be full equality for men and women.

# CHAPTER TWENTY THE IDEOLOGY OF FEMINISM

"Men are strong, logical, assertive, and independent and are meant to run the world and take care of their families. Women are weak, irrational, passive, and empty-headed and are happiest when they are taking care of children."

That simplistic belief is held by untold numbers of men and women and is the basis for the destructive "sex-role" system that has restricted the life choices of both sexes and prevented people from developing interests and goals that fulfill their own particular personalities and needs.

In *The American Dilemma,* Gunnar Myrdal's monumental book about racial discrimination published in 1944, a special appendix compares the myths that have grown up about blacks and women. Both have been said to have smaller brains and lack genius; both have been brought to believe in their own inferiority; both are accepted as long as they stay "in their place"; and in both cases, their oppressors have developed the myth that the victims are contented, said Myrdal. These similarities are not accidental, he wrote, but the result of the "paternalistic order of society." (Women and blacks also have both developed devious ways—shuffling for blacks, wiles for women—to get around "the Man.")

Psychiatrist Beatrice Hinkle writing in 1920 noted that, "It is generally regarded that a subject people are a retarded people no matter how kind their masters may be. For their proper development, the attitude and conditions of their environment must allow them unrestricted expression of their own qualities whether these agree with the preconceived ideas and wishes of the ruling class or not or even whether the subject people are satisfied with their own subjection." She protested against the assumption that women find their reason for being "not in any positive and individual contributions to the race but in fulfilling its purely animal functions and serving submissively and passively the needs and wishes of the superior beings, the males."

Wilma Scott Heide, the National Board Chairwoman of NOW and a behavioral scientist, said something similar fifty years later. "It is tragic," she told a Senate hearing on the Equal Rights Amendment, "that the reproductive abilities women share with all other mammals have been more highly valued and developed than the productive intelligence we do not share with any other animal."

The first step in the development of "sexism" was the definition of "masculinity" and "femininity" as two opposing concepts that described a world of psychological differences as well as a few physical ones—and which even overrated those physical differences when to do so was advantageous to men.

Somehow, all the psychological traits that men appropriated were the historical characteristics of master classes, and the traits assigned to women were those that were commonly descriptive of slaves.

One of the most astonishing was Freud's contention that women lacked a strong super-ego. That is, they had no strong sense of self. Freud never seemed to connect an apparent penchant for self-sacrifice with the culturally approved notion that "truly feminine" women ought to subordinate their own desires to those of their husbands and children. And if women were taught that it was feminine to put themselves last, that is just what they did. At any rate, it is rather difficult for any ego to develop when misogynists of the past and present insist that women have smaller brains, that women lack the psychological stamina for achievement, or that women who try to succeed in business or science or government or the arts are really evincing secret desires to be men.

The word "female" has come to be synonymous with sacrifice.

Women are supposed to defer to the wishes of men and devote themselves to their homes and children—and if they seek the fulfillment of their own potentials and personalities, they are called "selfish" and "unfeminine."

Women's egos are fettered and they accept as natural a kind of self-abnegation and submission that makes it certain they will never strike out for leadership or achievement. The world provides this lesson in many subtle ways. The fact that a woman takes a man's name dates from the time when a woman literally became his property. Most married women still submerge their identities in those of their husbands and the message communicated by a change of name is more than symbolic.

Women must come to believe that it is not "attractive" to be docile or submissive—that these characteristics are descriptive of slaves, not free human beings. Any man who seeks to dominate his wife or lover is showing his contempt for her individuality and humanity.

"Femininity." Does it have to do with the way a woman looks, the way she behaves, her goals and ambitions, the way she walks or talks, a certain style? Does feminine mean pretty? If so, most of the women in the world are not feminine—at least by movie star and fashion magazine standards. Does it mean quiet and unassuming and subservient? If so, most women with any intelligence or ambition are ruled out—and anyone who never opens her mouth qualifies!

Is physical weakness feminine? Does it require that one never engage in active sports—are girls or women who play softball or field hockey unfeminine? Or would they be more "feminine" if they engaged in acceptable sports like tennis and skiing? And what makes them acceptable? What makes a sport "masculine" or "feminine"?

The brain has no sex. Neither does the heart or mind or soul or whatever it is that makes people want to direct their lives in one direction or another. But there is something that makes one individual want to be a high school teacher, another an engineer, a third a nurse, and a fourth a business executive—and it has nothing whatsoever to do with the nature of his or her genitals. It has to do with culture.

Society tells children from the time they can understand that it is "masculine" to be an engineer and "feminine" to be a nurse. It is "masculine" to be aggressive and "feminine" to be yielding. When you analyze what is masculine and what is feminine in this society, you discover that it is "masculine" to control and direct and it is "feminine" to serve and take orders.

One study of women executives showed that many of them did not assert themselves at times when it was in their best interests to do so, because they were afraid of being considered "unfeminine." Women who are interested in medicine often become nurses rather than doctors because that is the "feminine" thing to do. One study showed that girls did much better at mathematics when the problems were posed in terms of cooking recipes rather than in traditional forms.

According to one bit of sexist propaganda, women are good at dull, repetitive jobs, and are better than men at tasks that require nimbleness and dexterity—thus the women file clerks and typists and the women who assemble complex circuitry at electronics plants. Ironically, when the typewriter was first invented, only men were hired as typists because it was decided that the machine was too *complex* for women. And where is the argument about feminine dexterity when it comes to training surgeons? In fact, many medical schools freely admit that they do not accept women students on an equal basis with men.

Are women intrinsically less intelligent than men? More emotional? Apt to go to pieces in a crisis? Unable to make decisions? Do they prefer a strong hand to guide them? During the bombing raids the Germans carried out against England in World War II, there were 70 percent more cases of emotional shock, hysteria, and psychoneurosis among men than women. The same was true in the concentration camps where women proved far more able to undergo mental stress and suffered breakdowns far less often than men. In simulated space flights conducted by the National Aeronautics and Space Administration (NASA) women demonstrated superior ability to endure the psychological hazards of space flight—and they were also better able to orient themselves to the spaceship and handle the controls. The Russians must agree, for they chose Valentina Tereshkova Nikolayeva to be the world's first woman astronaut.

Actually, though men are physically stronger, women are *constitutionally* stronger than men. They live longer and are better able to endure illness, exposure, fatigue, and starvation. Men are more susceptible to most disease; they are twenty-five or thirty times more likely to have heart attacks. A study of Catholic monks and nuns who lived similar kinds of lives showed that this is not due to the different kinds of work men and women do: the sisters lived five and one-half years longer than the monks.

Women are also emotionally more stable. Men outnumber women in mental institutions, and their suicide rate is about four times as high. They have four times as many stomach ulcers, have more nervous breakdowns, are the large majority of alcoholics, have been shown by tests to lose their temper more often, and are generally emotionally weaker than women.

Anthropologist Ashley Montagu suggests that part of the problem is that men have been taught to keep their emotions all bottled up. "Women," he says, "use their emotions a great deal more efficiently than men and not in the 'emotional' manner that men imply when they use the word disparagingly in connection with women. In this sense, women are positively *less* emotional than men."

Men suffer from the sexist stereotypes and false images of "masculinity." Boys and men are forced to act aggressive and belligerent when they may at heart be gentle and noncombative. From the time a boy is barely out of the toddler's stage, he learns that it is "sissy" to run away from a fight. Somehow, it is "masculine" to beat somebody up.

Bigger boys run into the same dilemma—and some of them solve it by "proving" their masculinity in wars. Or they get into barroom fights. Or they abuse their wives and children. Or they get vicarious thrills by watching boxing matches or football games. And even when being masculine does not require outright fisticuffs, it requires physical skill or prowess. So the captain of the football team becomes the school hero and the youth who is immersed in English literature or baroque music is considered somewhat strange—after all, his classmates say, those activities are "for girls."

As a result, the boy who is fascinated by such prohibited interests begins to feel that there is something not quite right with him. Even his parents often push him to go out and play baseball or exercise with weights, and if they live in a private home they may install a basketball hoop over the garage.

Try to make a list of what you consider "feminine." Then make a list of "masculine" traits. Do all the girls and boys or men and women you know fit nicely into one category or the other? Are the ones that do not fit really misfits? Dr. John Anderson of the Institute of Child Development and Welfare at the University of Michigan says that for virtually every psychological trait, the difference between the average male and female is only *one-tenth* as great as the range of differences among men or among women. This means that at the extremes, it may well be that the strongest or most aggressive person one can find is a man and the weakest, most yielding one a woman, but in between that will be a range of men and women who comfortably overlap.

And we do not know to what degree the existing differences between men and women are imposed by culture and training. We have been so brainwashed about "femininity" and "masculinity" that the words might better be banished from the language. After all, "feminine" and "masculine" are only words that describe a person's sex—nothing more. We might just as well say "female" and "male."

People are beginning to break down some of those stereotypes. Even "unisex" clothing and boys wearing long hair contribute to the idea that it is not always so essential to draw stark distinctions between males and females.

The supposed psychological and physical differences between men and women—the special nature of "masculinity" and "femininity"—have been used to establish a system of sex roles that restrict and limit the life choices of both men and women.

As a result of their "nurturing" qualities, women are supposed to be specially suited for caring for children. Somehow, doing the housework also goes along with the bargain, though elbow grease and stamina seem more relevant to domestic chores than any of the "mothering" qualities women are supposed to have.

The housework battle is significant for two reasons—one, because it has kept overworked women from exploring their potential in other areas, and two, because it labels domestic chores as female duties with the unstated assumption that they are beneath the dignity of men. If women are the ones who do such demeaning chores, they must be inferior beings.

Feminist poet Kay Reinartz makes her comment about the lot of housewives with this pointed turnabout:

"*Domesticity*"

*His back is bowed from the endless hours of toil*
*his body reeks of the sweat that is man's badge of*
*virtuous occupation*

*Around the wide expanse of his paunch is twisted*
*a bit of bright colored cloth*
*his banner of pride and defeat?*

*For him there is no life but that of continual service*
*and his days and nights placed end to end*
*stretch out in a narrow, grey, endless ribbon*
*stretching from here to*

*n*
*o*
*w*
*h*
*e*
*r*
*e*
*he is*
*the househusband.*

Incidentally, there's no apparent "nurturing" reason for a woman to stay home and keep house *before* she has children, but that flows from the other side of the motherhood myth—that a woman's *only* important job in life is to bear and raise children. Therefore, if her husband can earn enough for the two of them, there's no real reason she should work.

Women are not expected or encouraged to achieve in this society. Samuel Johnson in the 1600's said that "a woman's preaching is like a dog's walking on his hinder legs. It is not done well; but you are surprised to find it done at all." And he also said, "A man is better pleased when he has a good dinner upon his table than when his wife talks Greek."

Obviously, the role of woman, according to past and present sexists, is not to achieve anything in her own right but to serve men. A wife serves her husband, a nurse serves the doctor, a secretary serves her boss, and on down the line.

Whatever job a wife does, it is considered less important than her husband's and, for the benefit of his "ego" (that really means his sense of superiority) her job had better pay less as well. Rampant sex discrimination makes that rather likely anyway.

If a man gets a job offer in another city, his wife should move to be with him, says the culture. But if that means she has to leave a job she likes—or if *she* gets a chance for advancement out of town—well, those missed opportunities are just tucked away in her memory book. The man is "the provider" and therefore, his job and advancement are the only considerations. Women who protest this sexist notion are called "selfish" and "unfeminine"—charged with wanting to compete with their husbands.

Feminists decry the idea that what a woman does is unimportant or that her only necessary role is to care for children and keep house. In fact, feminists protest the belief that those are "women's jobs" in the first place. They see no "men's" or "women's" jobs aside from the special roles each sex plays in conception and childbirth. The way society has set up the roles, however, women often have to choose between careers and children; even if they have careers, mothers must restrict their work to areas that do not conflict with their home chores. Men never have to make those choices.

Women should not have to either. It is rarely necessary for a pregnant woman to take off more than a month before giving birth and a few weeks afterward. Unless women start breeding like rabbits, that only means a few months out of a lifetime. (One out of ten married women have no children at all.) The conflict with work is not giving birth to the child, but caring for it. And feminists say *that* job should be shared by *both* parents.

After the birth, of course, some arrangement for child care must be made—a housekeeper or relative, an infant-care center, or some agreement whereby the man and woman both have part-time jobs, work alternately for certain months or years at a time, or decide that one person, mother or father, will stop working and stay home.

Immediately, clamorous voices cry, "But you can't have the man work part time or at specific periods of time that he alternates with his wife! What will happen to his career!" A good question—but why don't people ask what will happen to his wife's career, if she is forced to withdraw from her work completely? Why is it that we assume it is all right for a woman to sacrifice her career, but believe it unthinkable in a man?

Other antifeminist critics declare that it is somehow "natural" for a woman to stay home and care for children, while a man works to support them. The word "natural" has an invidious habit of appearing whenever somebody wants to prove that something is necessary even when it is harmful.

The concept of natural motherhood, of course, dates from the time that women were condemned to perpetual childbearing by the lack of contraception, when extreme sex discrimination made it impossible to get work outside the home other than as maids, governesses, factory workers, or prostitutes—all jobs that were degrading and paid little. None of this was especially "good" for women, though people at the time argued that it was all very "natural."

Even modern childbirth is no longer "natural" in its literal sense. After all, babies are delivered by trained obstetricians and watched over in their early days by pediatricians. And if motherhood comes so naturally, why all those baby books that have sales in the millions? It should all be instinctive. Moreover, the baby doctors are usually men; it doesn't seem to be "unnatural" for a man to be involved with the care of children as long as he gets paid for it.

The role of compulsory child rearer and housekeeper not only deprives women of realizing their individual potentials as creative human beings, but also establishes a system in which women must live through their husbands and families. This can lead to oppressive relationships in which a woman seeks to establish control over her family's private activities. One writer said children seem to suffer from "smother love." Feminists think it is better for everyone if a woman is more than "Charlie's wife" and "Susie's mother." The role of a woman has to be more than taking care of other people.

The sex-role system robs a woman of her identity. In this society, women are defined by men. Their own status in the community is determined largely by their husbands' achievements, and even when they receive recognition in their own right, newspapers identify them as Mrs. John Jones. Imagine a man being called *Mr.* Sarah Bumblemeyer! And while a man who is not married is called a carefree bachelor, women who are single are failures and old maids. Failure for a woman is not being chosen by a man.

Men also define women's own attitudes about themselves. A "feminine" woman is pleasing—and not threatening—to a man. A "good wife" supports her husband's ego and encourages him in his work. When businesses choose executives, frequently they interview a man's wife as well. Yet, it is not assumed that a husband should encourage a wife in her work in the same way—or make sacrifices to help her succeed. And since businesses largely refuse to employ women as executives, they don't have the opportunity to ask about husbands! In fact, one of the excuses given against promoting women is that they will have home responsibilities that will detract from their dedication to their jobs. With men it's just the other way around—their wives are expected to arrange their lives to fit in with their husbands' work needs and schedules.

Men also define what is considered "womanly" and "feminine." Those are adjectives applied to women who are pliant, compliant, and anxious to please men and support their egos. A woman must practically efface herself to be "womanly" in this sense. Yet, women themselves are caught in this myth and they measure themselves as well as others against the same sexist standards.

Ultimately, according to the male definition of "true womanhood," women exist for men—to please them and serve them, to create a "snug harbor" where they can retreat from the world outside, to make them feel important, to bear their children. And in return, the man makes his wife feel that she is fulfilling her womanly functions—that she is realizing her destiny. Except that somehow it does not always work.

One of the largest sources of patients for the couches of American psychoanalysts are the suburban housewives who feel empty and useless and wonder if this is really all life is about. Others who never get to the analysts' offices experience the same malaise. Unfortunately, they often get bad advice about "adjusting" to their "feminine role."

One author actually advised that dissatisfied housewives learn to bake their own bread!

Even if a woman is in the work world, she sees the reflections of discrimination all around her. Men run things, women aid and serve them. Men do the important things while the majority of wives do domestic work and care for children—jobs with so little value in the society that the people who do them professionally are among the worst paid of workers. When were servants ever considered superior to their masters? So a woman comes out thinking that somehow it is right that men run corporations and governments, because she would not be capable.

All of this has its destructive effect on women. Many limit their own ambitions. They do not take themselves seriously. They begin to think they are lucky to be cared for, because they really could not "make it" alone. Many develop contempt for other women. Many women in movement "rap" sessions have admitted that they never liked other women. They thought women were dull and uninteresting and they preferred the company of men. This sense of inferiority and contempt for women easily leads to self-hatred.

Aside from wife and mother, the other role women have been schooled to play is sex object. Women are taught that their most prized assets are a good figure and pretty face, while men become desirable when they achieve power or riches or acclaim. Thus women dread growing old and losing their looks; they make pitiful jokes about their ages ("twenty-one plus") and sometimes they are literally cast off by husbands looking for younger companions.

Today, in an era when contraception and abortion make it possible for women to avoid pregnancy and childbirth, a new sexual revolution has occurred. Though remnants of the old double standard still exist, at least in this country, women do not face the penalties that exist in some Muslim countries where women guilty of adultery are *still* stoned to death.

However, feminists are concerned that the new sexual freedom should not become a new means of exploitation of women—that women should not be forced into sex merely because it is the thing to do and that they should not be treated as sexual objects today in the same way that prostitutes have been treated as sexual objects throughout history. It will be no great victory to extend that exploitation to the female population at large. Feminists do not want the return of the time when women did not have the right to say "yes," but they insist that the mores of society give women the right to say "no."

Women are turned into sex objects both vulgarly and subtly. They are the objects of catcalls and once-over glances in the street. The once-over is not much more comfortable in offices or at parties when some males act as if they would like to reconstruct the old slave markets where auctioneers commented on a woman's best parts as if they were showing prize horses. The supposedly hip new life-styles that are defined by rock music and "turning on" are just as exploitative of women as the square ones. Although both men and women may have long hair and live in "pads," it is still the female doing the housework and the male doing "his thing,"—which is obviously considered more important than "her thing."

One woman on a job interview told how the man interviewing her kept commenting on how much he liked her body rather than talking about her professional qualifications. One woman television reporter has become so outraged at being treated like a sex object instead of a colleague that she deliberately ignores personal compliments about her looks or dress. Perhaps these are extremes, but they are symptomatic of the humiliation many women are forced to suffer.

Books, movies, other media, and advertising reflect and reinforce the message. Advertising is probably the worst offender. When the woman who has dyed her hair or used "Brand X" face cream is seen being admired by some handsome man, copywriters refer to him as "the male reward." In addition, the ads also tell a woman about her other roles—Did you ever see a man washing dishes or doing the laundry? In ads, men are the ones who give the instructions. Advertising agency executives say that this is done deliberately because "men have the voice of authority." Even in the kitchen, where according to advertisers a woman spends most of her life, she needs a man to tell her what to do!

Pornography and "girlie" magazines are the worst of a genre, but the kind of magazines you will find in a dentist's waiting room use women's bodies to sell cars, cigarettes, airline tickets—even business machines. One incredible ad for Dictaphone calculators suggested that the machine was so simple to operate, even a woman could do it. The copy said, "Our new line of calculators goes through its final ordeal. The dumb blonde test."

An ad for Iberia Airlines hinted that the stewardess would be full of extra little surprises. "This nice little blonde from Barcelona will romance you all the way to Spain. And England. And France . . ." etc. An ad for Parker Pen topped them all. It showed a teen-age girl lying on her bed with a puzzled, distraught expression. "You might as well give her a gorgeous pen to keep her checkbook unbalanced with," said the copy. "A sleek and shining pen will make her feel prettier. Which is more important to any girl than solving mathematical mysteries."

Some companies *are* becoming sensitive to feminist protests. The firm that manufactures Toyota automobiles agreed to withdraw an ad that showed a young man on a beach carrying a surfboard and eyeing a station wagon full of bikini-clad women. The copy said: "You can fit a lot of important things in a Toyota Wagon." Toyota received a NOW "Barefoot and Pregnant Award" objecting to the portrayal of women as sex objects. A company spokesman replied, "We've agreed that this is not the type of ad we want to do. I'm pretty sure we're going to be a little more careful in the future about the kind of ads we run."

Even some of the women who have been caught in the sex symbol role are beginning to rebel. Wendy Dascomb, Miss America of 1969, declared, "You're like an animal and everybody's staring at you up and down and back up again." She called the experience "instant zoo." And Karen Johnson, a runner-up in the 1970 Miss America contest exclaimed, "You expect the judges to stand up and stamp 'U.S. Inspected Red Horsemeat' on your hip."

"But, don't you want men to light your cigarettes and open doors for you?" come the earnest queries. The chivalry game is deceptive and dangerous—the suffragists know that.

A "chivalrous" man may help his wife on with her coat—a task she could obviously do herself and that is more for show than anything else (He is more likely to do it in a restaurant where people can see than in the privacy of their home)—but he is quite unlikely to volunteer to do the much more physically taxing work of cleaning the house.

And the men who say that if women want equal rights they must give up the "privileges of chivalry" are saying, in effect, that those courtesies were not given to them because they were women but because they were inferior.

As one feminist said, "The doors that are opened don't make up for all the doors that are shut." And the free dinners in restaurants women eat hardly represent a fraction of the difference in pay they would get if they were the same sex as their escorts. When men pay for women, they are saying very clearly that they have been earning more and have more earning power—another comment on female inferiority.

Think of the last novel you read or the latest movie you've seen. What were the women like and what were their relationships to men? Was it a love story where the woman's sole aim was to catch her man? Or was there an added twist—did a "cold, hard, career woman" type decide to give it all up for love? (Her love didn't have to give up *his* career, did he?) Was she a dumb, flighty, willowy blonde who wore necklines down to her navel and provided the sex interest? Was she just an accessory to the plot, a kind of girl Friday who did useful errands and glowed adoringly whenever the hero said a kind word or looked in her direction?

Or perhaps she was a vicious "man eating" bitch or a castrating wife or a domineering mother. You can probably add some other examples to the list of female charmers that have been devised. The key point, of course, is that virtually all plays and movies and the majority of novels are written by men who are free to give vent to their own prejudices or conflicts about women. It is seldom that a woman can find a fictional female with whom she can identify or who seems to speak to her own problems.

Television repeats all the stereotypes in comedy and drama, and through its news broadcasts, it reinforces the image of a world where women have little importance. Except for one or two token women, the news staffs are all male—including the "anchormen" and commentators. (Television executives assert that women's voices lack "credibility.") And they talk of a world where the only important happenings are directed by men. Women seem to do little except worry about fashion and, maybe, education. The same is true of newspapers, although since salaries are lower, women have made more progress there—though not on the level of editorial decision-making.

The reports of the women's rights movement have frequently been sarcastic and patronizing. It was television and newspapers that perpetrated the hoax about "bra burning" (it never actually happened), so that they could treat the movement as a joke and avoid coming to terms with its significance. As a result, they have acted to shift attention away from its real demands. Newspaper "women's pages" are as insulting as the women's auxiliaries in political parties. A newsletter published by the Albuquerque, New Mexico, chapter of NOW printed this true but tongue-in-cheek story on "The Men's Page":

> *Former State Senator Sterling Black of Los Alamos was the guest speaker at the May 3 meeting of the National Organization for Women.*
>
> *A handsome, elderly man with silver-gray hair and delicately masculine features, Senator Black wore a conservative dark-brown suit with a lemon-yellow shirt, a platinum wedding ring and matching watch, and an ivory and maroon tie with a double row of gold links across it. His voice is low and pleasant, but compelling.*
>
> *Senator Black's wife is Dr. Nancy Black, a clinical psychologist now practicing in Portales, New Mexico.*

There are no "men's pages" in American newspapers—one assumes that the majority of the paper is for men, and that women should be largely concerned with engagement notices, recipes, charity balls, and fashion.

What is the way out of this sexist system that is based on cultural beliefs that are thousands of years old?

There are many different paths, and in the years ahead, different people and organizations will tread them, wearing deep ruts in some when they run up against intransigence and moving easily over other paths when they meet with support and agreement.

There is the political route. Women will seek new legislation in areas like equal opportunity for education and employment, child care, abortion, and legal rights. They will file court suits and complaints with government agencies to protest violations of existing laws and policies. They will seek to elect both male and female legislators who promote the cause of women's rights.

They will also seek to educate the public with meetings and conferences, by demonstrating and picketing, by appearing on radio and television, by writing books and articles, and by interminable conversations over coffee cups and backyard fences, at water coolers and corner drugstores, in offices and schools and factories and everywhere that people meet.

There is also another route—perhaps even more difficult—and that involves making feminist principles the basis for one's own personal life. But even that is beginning to happen.

Feminist couples—and those who just agree with the fairness of the idea—are sharing household chores and child rearing. One couple, both university professors, alternate the days of their classes, so that one can be home to take care of the children. Another husband and wife each works part time, one in the morning, the other in the afternoon, so they can share the care of the new baby. A young graduate student does his share of cooking, cleaning, and ironing so his wife can devote more of her energies to her job as a book editor.

A newspaper story about the effect of women's liberation on family life told of a forty-two-year-old woman from Cleveland who sat her husband and children down and let them know what she thought about "getting stuck with all the dirty jobs." "They hadn't understood how I felt, but there aren't any boys' jobs or girls' jobs anymore. Now the boys work in the kitchen. Once nobody could feed himself if I wasn't home to cook. That was my job. Now *if I'm not home,* my husband cooks dinner himself." (Well, that is partial liberation!)

In some cases, feminist women have found their husbands or boyfriends completely intransigent. There is no easy answer for that kind of situation, except that, increasingly, women are refusing to put up with men who demean or exploit them. A handful advocate severing all personal relationships with men. Most, slightly more optimistic, hope that there are some men around who do not feel their masculinity threatened by a woman who seeks to be treated as an equal rather than as an inferior.

For single women, an act of personal liberation may be paying their own way on dates—though others feel that as long as men earn twice as much as women, paying the check is a mild form of reparation! (Elizabeth Cady Stanton favored "going Dutch" and said the existing system degraded women.) Or they may call men instead of waiting to be called, thus removing the male's powerful advantage in social situations. And they will hopefully refuse to let themselves be used or abused and think that they are performing some "natural" supportive function. Ultimately, the struggle for personal liberation is likely to be the most important one of all.

But how about you? What are the implications of women's liberation and of everything you have read in this book on *your* life and *your* plans for the future? You are going to have to decide whether you will live according to the traditional patterns of the sex-role system or whether you will discard them.

If you are a girl in school now, do you take yourself and your work seriously? Do you worry that if you seem too smart, boys will not like you? Do you have ambitions for the future? Have you limited your thinking to the traditional "women's" careers? Where do marriage and family fit in your life? Will they be everything or only part of a future that includes work and hobbies and other outside interests? Do you think it is necessary for you to have children? If you marry, do you think your future husband's interests ought to come before yours? Do you think you will be a failure if you do not get married at all?

Perhaps it is too early to answer all of these questions. Certainly, teen-age girls do not have to decide immediately whether they are going to get married and have children. However, there are some other decisions you ought to begin making, decisions about your attitude toward yourself and your goals for the future. If you believe that your needs and desires are as valid as those of anyone on this earth, you will never let yourself accept conditions that limit your humanity or deny your own needs for satisfaction and fulfillment.

You may decide to follow the traditional housewife-mother role. And, with the spread of feminist ideas, *so may some men*. Perhaps that will no longer be solely a woman's role, but a life-style available to anyone regardless of sex.

The most important thing is that you understand the alternatives and the implications they will have for the rest of your life—and that you have a choice as free as that of the boy who may be sitting in the classroom seat next to you. That is the goal and the promise of women's liberation.

# SUGGESTIONS FOR ADDITIONAL READING

*Recommended Reading*

Bettelheim, Bruno. *The Children of the Dream.* New York: Macmillan, 1969—describes the results of communal child rearing on the Israeli kibbutz.

Bird, Caroline. *Born Female.* New York: Pocket Books, 1969 (paperback)—a survey of the kinds of job discrimination women face.

Brophy, Brigid. *Don't Never Forget.* New York: Holt, 1966—clever, pointed essays on the status of women.

De Beauvoir, Simone. *The Second Sex.* New York: Bantam, 1968 (paperback)—an attempt to explain the historical status of women as "the other"—the opposite of man—by using history, mythology, literature, and biology. Complex and sometimes difficult.

Ferguson, Charles. *The Male Attitude.* Boston: Little, Brown, 1966—men have been taught they must be aggressive and combative in order to be "masculine."

Flexner, Eleanor. *Century of Struggle.* New York: Atheneum, 1968 (paperback)—the history of women's struggle in America, including chapters on education, labor unions, and the fight for suffrage.

Friedan, Betty. *The Feminine Mystique.* New York: Dell, 1964 (paperback)—a study of the reasons for the unhappiness and frustration of women who have given up possible careers to become full-time housewives.

Gornick, Vivian and Moran, Barbara K., eds. *Woman in Sexist Society.*

New York: Basic Books, 1971—essays by modern feminists on the role of women in society.

Kraditor, Aileen, ed. *Up from the Pedestal.* Chicago: Quadrangle, 1970 (paperback)—writings of the early feminist movement in America. A good sampling.

Lessing, Doris. *The Golden Notebook.* New York: Ballantine, 1968 (paperback)—novel about the struggle for fulfillment of a woman writer.

Ludovici, L. J. *The Final Inequality.* New York: Norton, 1965—a view of the historical subjugation of women with interesting sections about misogyny.

Mead, Margaret. *Male and Female.* New York: Dell, 1968 (paperback)—shows that the notions of the duties and characteristics assigned to each sex are different in cultures around the world.

Millet, Kate. *Sexual Politics.* Garden City: Doubleday, 1970—a discussion of the subjugation of women with a special emphasis on misogyny in literature.

Nin, Anais. *Ladders to Fire.* Chicago: Swallow, 1959 (paperback)—novel about a woman who rejects the traditional "feminine" role.

Woolf, Virginia. *A Room of One's Own.* New York. Harcourt, Brace, 1929—a beautifully written essay on the difficulties faced by women who seek achievement in the professional world.

### *Other Books on Women*

Adams, Mildred. *The Right to Be People.* New York: Lippincott, 1967—the story of the struggle for women's suffrage in America.

Beard, Mary. *Women As a Force in History.* New York: Collier,—— (paperback)—a review of the legal status of women at various times.

Epstein, Cynthia Fuchs. *Woman's Place.* Berkeley: University of California, 1970—account of the problems women face in employment.

Firestone, Shulamith. *The Dialectic of Sex.* New York: Morrow, 1970—the theory of radical feminism by a member of the new movement.

Gilman, Charlotte Perkins. *Women and Economics.* New York: Harper, 1966 (paperback)—women must be economically independent of men and should not be forced to stay in the home; first published in 1898.

Hardin, Garrett. *Population, Evolution and Birth Control.* San Francisco: Freeman, 1969—historical retrospective of attitudes toward abortion and birth control.

Hayes, H. R. *The Dangerous Sex: The Myth of Feminine Evil.* New York: Pocket Books, 1965 (paperback)—men's fear of women throughout history.

Merriam, Eve. *After Nora Slammed the Door.* Cleveland: World, 1962—incisive essays on the woman question.

Montagu, Ashley. *The Natural Superiority of Women.* New York: Collier, 1970 (paperback)—somewhat patronizing book that nevertheless has some interesting material in the areas of biology and psychology.

Morgan, Robin, ed. *Sisterhood Is Powerful.* New York: Vintage, 1970 (paperback)—writings from the women's liberation movement.

Rossi, Alice, ed. *Essays on Sex Equality by John Stuart Mill and Harriet Taylor Mill.* Chicago: University of Chicago, 1971—includes J. S. Mill's "On the Subjection of Women."

Wollstonecraft, Mary. *A Vindication of the Rights of Women.* New York: Norton, 1967 (paperback)—a plea for equality written in 1791; the eighteenth century language is sometimes tedious, but it is amazing to see a woman who lived two hundred years ago make the feminist arguments that are made today.

# INDEX

## THE WOMEN WHO CREATED THIS BOOK

The author of *The New Feminism,* free-lance writer Lucy Komisar was elected 1969–1970 vice-president of the National Organization for Women. She became a feminist as the result of widespread discrimination she encountered while seeking employment as a journalist. At one interview she was told outright, "I'm sorry, but we already have three *girls.*"

Ms. Komisar was graduated from Queens College of the City University of New York in 1964 with a B.A. in history. For a year she served as a special assistant to the deputy administrator of the Human Resources Administration in New York and was press secretary in the successful primary campaign of former Congressman Allard Lowenstein.

In 1962–63, she was editor of the *Mississippi Free Press,* a pro-civil-rights weekly published in Jackson. She worked as a reporter and associate producer for National Educational Television on news features and documentaries and has also been a writer, reporter, and producer for WBAI radio in New York City.

She has written cover stories for the *Saturday Review* ("The New Feminism"), *New York Magazine* ("The Arrogance of Power"), and the *Washington Monthly* ("Violence and the Masculine Mystique").

Some of the other women who helped to create *The New Feminism* are: Claudia Cohl, editor; Nancy Macomber, researcher; Joan Handelsman Greene, copy editor; Mary Kamins, proofreader; Addie West, editorial assistant; Gisela Knight, indexer; Judie Mills, designer; and Barbara Pfeffer Fishman, photographer. In addition, female employees of Vail-Ballou Press, Inc., worked to proofread printer's galleys and to coordinate production.